CANADIAN CONNECTIONS

KATHRYN E. GALVIN
with MARGARET BARRY

REIDMORE BOOKS

ABOUT THE AUTHORS

Kathryn Galvin is an elementary school assistant principal in Calgary. She received her undergraduate degree in education from the University of Calgary and is currently working on her master's degree at the same university, with a concentration in the area of social studies. Ms. Galvin has four years of consulting experience and has contributed to the *History and Social Science Teacher* periodical. She has published two textbooks and expects a third to be released in 1991. Ms. Galvin is very responsive to the needs of students and teachers and has an interesting and informative writing style that appeals to elementary students.

Margaret Barry is a full-time freelance writer and editor. She has authored several books, both trade and educational, and has contributed to numerous magazines, journals, and newspapers. Ms. Barry currently teaches non-fiction writing at the University of Alberta Extention Programme, and teaches communication, public speaking, and life-skills for Dr. Battle and Associates Consultants.

Reidmore Books would like to thank the following Academic Consultants for their advice regarding pedagogy, content, and curriculum development.

Dr. Don Massey, The University of Alberta
Dr. Roland Case, Faculty of Education, Simon Fraser University
Lesley Heppleston, Garneau Elementary School, Edmonton, Alberta
Bill Godfrey, Malmo Elementary School, Edmonton, Alberta

Canadian Cataloguing in Publication Data

Galvin, Kathryn E., 1951-

Canadian connections
ISBN 0-919091-97-0

1. Canada—Relations—Great Britain—Juvenile literature. 2. Canada—Relations—France—Juvenile literature. 3. Canada—Relations—United States—Juvenile literature. 4. Great Britain—Relations—Canada—Juvenile literature. 5. France—Relations—Canada—Juvenile literature. 6. United States—Relations—Canada—Juvenile literature. 7. Canada—Civilization—Foreign influences—Juvenile literature. I. Barry, Margaret, 1958—. II. Title.

FC242.G34 1991 j303.48'271 C90-091558-7
F1029.G34 1991

REIDMORE BOOKS INC.
Suite 012 Lemarchand Mansion
11523 - 100 Avenue
Edmonton, Alberta T5K 0J8

printed and bound in Canada

The Cover
The photographs on the cover show the four countries talked about in *Canadian Connections*. Match each photo with its country. Once you have read the book, look at the cover pictures again. They also show links between the countries. What are those links?

CONTENTS

CHAPTER 3
Canada—Through the Eyes of Others 38

CHAPTER 4
Transportation and Trade 50

CHAPTER 5
Modern Connections: Communication and Culture 68

CHAPTER 6
Canadian Contributions 84

INTRODUCTION

Have you ever moved or had someone new move into your neighbourhood? For the first few days, you can feel very alone. This feeling changes when there is a chance to get to know other people. This **interaction** may happen when you meet someone your own age. It is possible that you will become friends.

Friendship is a form of **link**. Friends will work and play together in a way that meets the needs of both people. When friends learn and grow together in positive ways, we can say they are a **positive influence** on each other.

There are also times when friends are not in agreement. If one person does something she thinks is wrong, just because her friends are doing it, the influence is negative. It may be better to break the link because it is not meeting the needs of each individual.

As you read on, you will often see the words **interaction**, **links**, and **influence** used. We can use these words to talk about what happens between people. Since countries are made up of people, we can also use these terms to talk about what happens between countries. The ideas work in the same way.

COUNTRIES

Canada is a large country. When we look at a map, we can see **borders** which show us where the lands of Canada begin and end. When we travel by land, we pass through border crossings which also show us where the lands of Canada begin and end. Borders mark the space where certain rules of living change.

Even though the rules change from one country to the next, we continue to travel back and forth, and to trade and share ideas. This book is about some of the ways that Canada shares ideas with three other countries. These countries are Great Britain, France, and the United States.

CARTOON PREVIEWS

Each chapter of *Canadian Connections* begins with a Cartoon Preview. There are four characters who introduce you to the subject of each of the chapters. The characters have been chosen with great care. Each character is the animal symbol of his country!

Canada's symbol is the beaver. In the cartoon stories, the beaver acts as the one who brings all of the others together. He tells them that Canada is made up of many peoples. Canada has many links.

The beaver, lion, rooster, and bald eagle are symbols for their countries.

The bald eagle is the symbol for the United States. His point of view is American.

Great Britain's symbol is the lion. What does the lion mean to you? As you read, think about all of the animal characters.

The rooster is the symbol for France. He tells you about France and the people of France. All of the animal characters tell you about some of the things that are important to Canada.

GETTING READY TO READ

As you read this book, you will see a number of symbols called **icons**. Each icon signals that you will be asked to get actively involved in your learning. The **Icon Guide** on the next page will introduce you to the gathering, organizing, and sharing strategies you will be using in this book.

At the beginning of each chapter, you will find a **Preview Page**. This page will give you an introduction to the main ideas in the chapter. At the end of each chapter, watch for a **Chapter Wrap-Up**. The **Activities** described will give you a chance to try out some of the things you are learning.

You will find a number of words in bold type in *Canadian Connections*. These may be words you have not seen or used before. If you are unsure of one of these words, you can find the meaning in the alphabetical **Glossary** at the end of this book.

ICON GUIDE

Gathering, organizing, and sharing information works best when we have a number of different strategies. As you use this book, you will be introduced to several strategies. These strategies, or ways of using information, are listed below. Each way has its own icon, including one you design yourself!

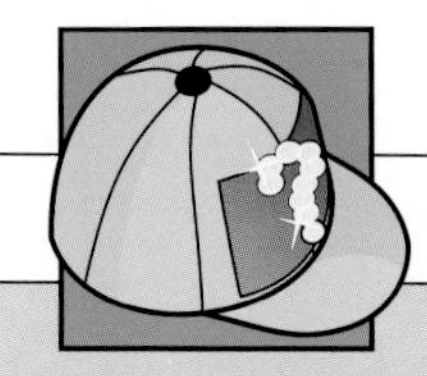

THINKING CAP

At the sign of the Thinking Cap you will have the opportunity to organize ideas in your mind. Strategies you will learn about are brainstorming, webbing, and forming questions.

PERSONAL JOURNAL

As you use *Canadian Connections*, you will be asked to do some writing. Use your Personal Journal to keep all of this writing in one place. Personal journals are a way to record and work with new ideas.

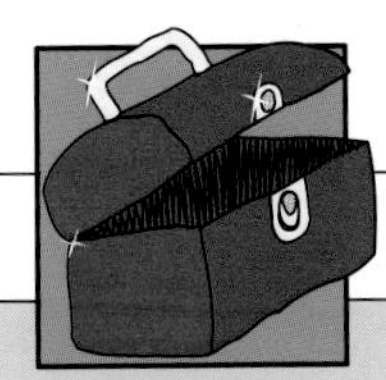

TOOLBOX

The Toolbox is a "how to" guide to help you try out some strategies on your own.

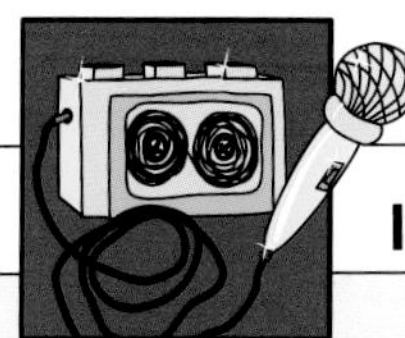

INTERVIEW & SURVEY

An Interview allows you to collect information by talking directly to people. A Survey allows you to collect information from people either by talking to them or by having them answer a question sheet.

MAPS

A Map is a type of overhead diagram showing information about a place or large area.

REPORT WRITING & OUTLINING

Writing a Report is one way to share factual information with others. Reports can include maps, diagrams, charts, and other visuals. The first step in Writing a Report is to decide on some research questions or to draft an Outline.

EDITORIAL

An Editorial is a way of giving your opinion in writing. Editorials are included in most newspapers.

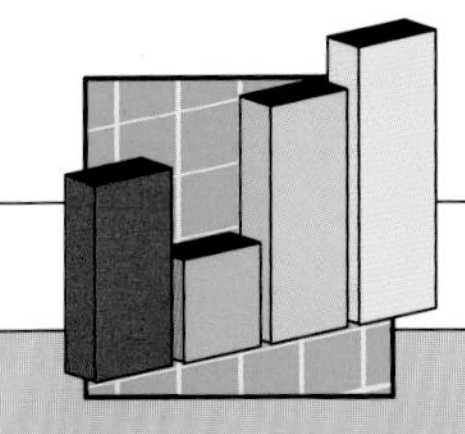

CHARTS & GRAPHS

Charts and Graphs organize information without using sentences and paragraphs. Charts help us compare information. Graphs help us get a "picture" of the information.

DESIGN YOUR OWN ICON

There are some activities that will ask you to Design Your Own Icon as a part of what you are doing. Keep in mind that an icon should represent what the activity is doing. Have fun!

CHAPTER 1

LAND AND SEA

PREVIEW PAGE

In this chapter you will read about the location of the three countries under study. It helps to have a picture in your mind of the places you are reading about. This chapter is designed to help you form that image: there are many colourful photographs!

You will use a diagram to help you sort out the countries, continents, and provinces. These terms are part of the language used to describe world connections.

Canada is connected with many countries. Our land has been linked to Great Britain, France, and the United States since before Canada became a country. You will use a map to locate these three countries. Potpourri pages show you images of the three countries. You might want to make a potpourri page of your own for Canada.

PERSONAL JOURNAL

1. In your personal journal, you will want to record data about Canada. As one way to begin this chapter, write down 10 things that make a person Canadian.

Have you ever thought about what it means to be a Canadian? In *Canadian Connections*, you will discover and explore the influences that have helped to shape our country. You will study the impact that Great Britain, France, and the United States have had in forming our Canadian identity. In turn, you will also review how Canadian contributions to these countries, and to the world, have affected Canada's ties to them.

In *Canadian Connections* we will look at

- Canada's physical relationship to Britain, France, and the United States.
- How Canada's past has affected our present.
- Stories that illustrate how Canadians, British, French, and Americans view their differences and similarities.
- Transportation and trade ties between Canada and these three countries.
- Canadians who have made important contributions to the world.

You will be given many opportunities to ask questions and learn about Canada and these three countries through a variety of interesting activities. After reading *Canadian Connections*, and completing your activities, you will have a better understanding of how Canada is connected to these countries.

Many times throughout the year, people from different countries come together. They show the flags of their countries. When do countries come together?

WORLD CONNECTIONS

Have you ever wondered about the way the world seems to fit together? If you have, you are like most people. Many people have difficulty seeing how the puzzle of the world works. Let's take some time to see if we can make the connections a little clearer. This diagram may help you see how it all fits together.

Countries, continents, provinces! All these terms are used to explain the way our world is organized. Each of the countries in our study have special features. Their landscapes, cities, and seasides are all different.

Great Britain is made up of islands. They are surrounded by the Atlantic Ocean and the North Sea. The English Channel connects France with Great Britain. France also has **coast** along the Atlantic Ocean and the Mediterranean Sea.

The Atlantic Ocean connects Canada and the United States with Great Britain and France. The United States and Canada are on the same continent, called North America. When places are connected by physical features, like the English Channel or the Atlantic Ocean, we can say they are linked.

In the following pages you will look at a map of the world. In later chapters, you will have an opportunity to "visit" three countries. Where are these countries in the world? Let's look at the map to find out!

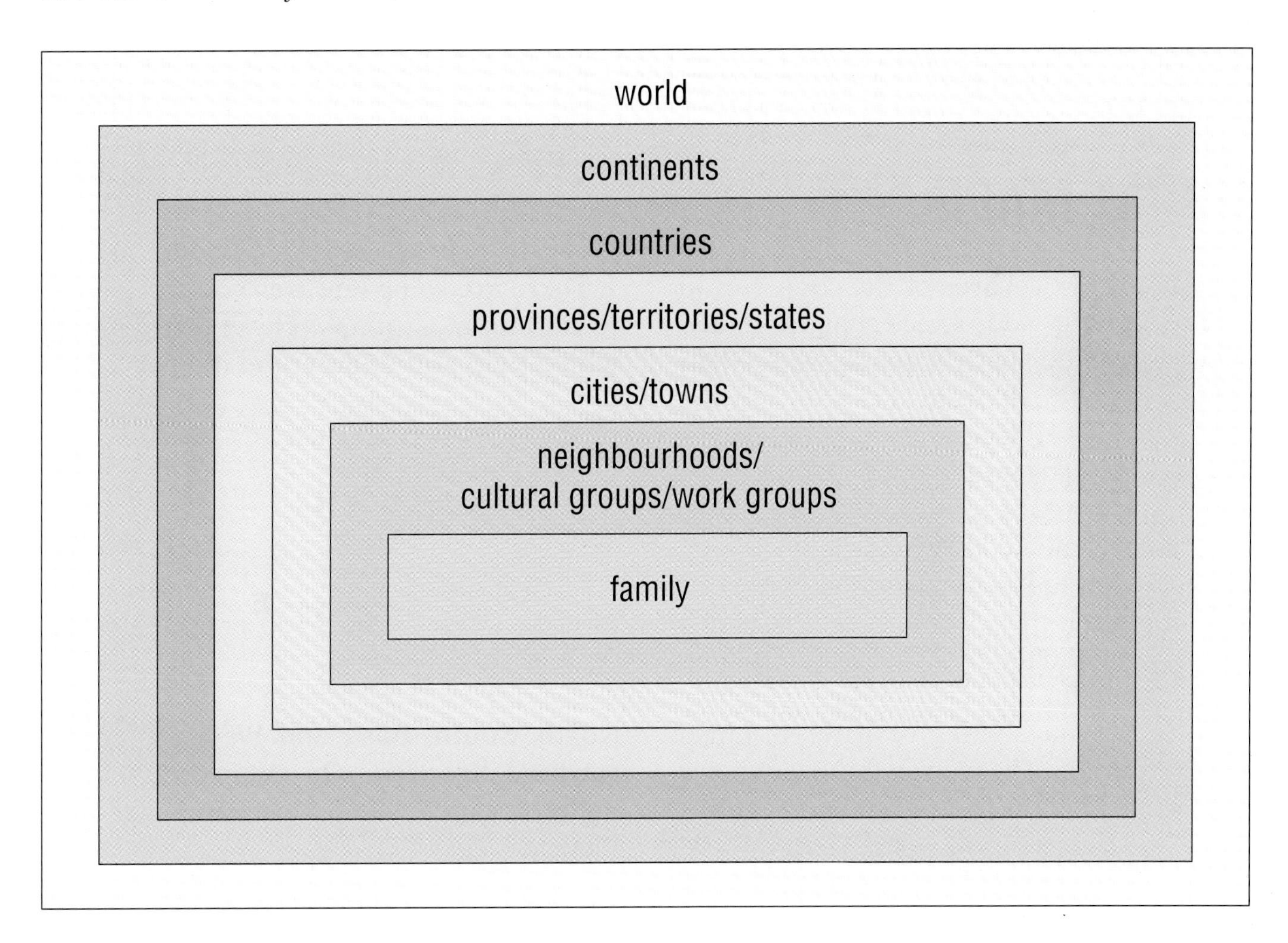

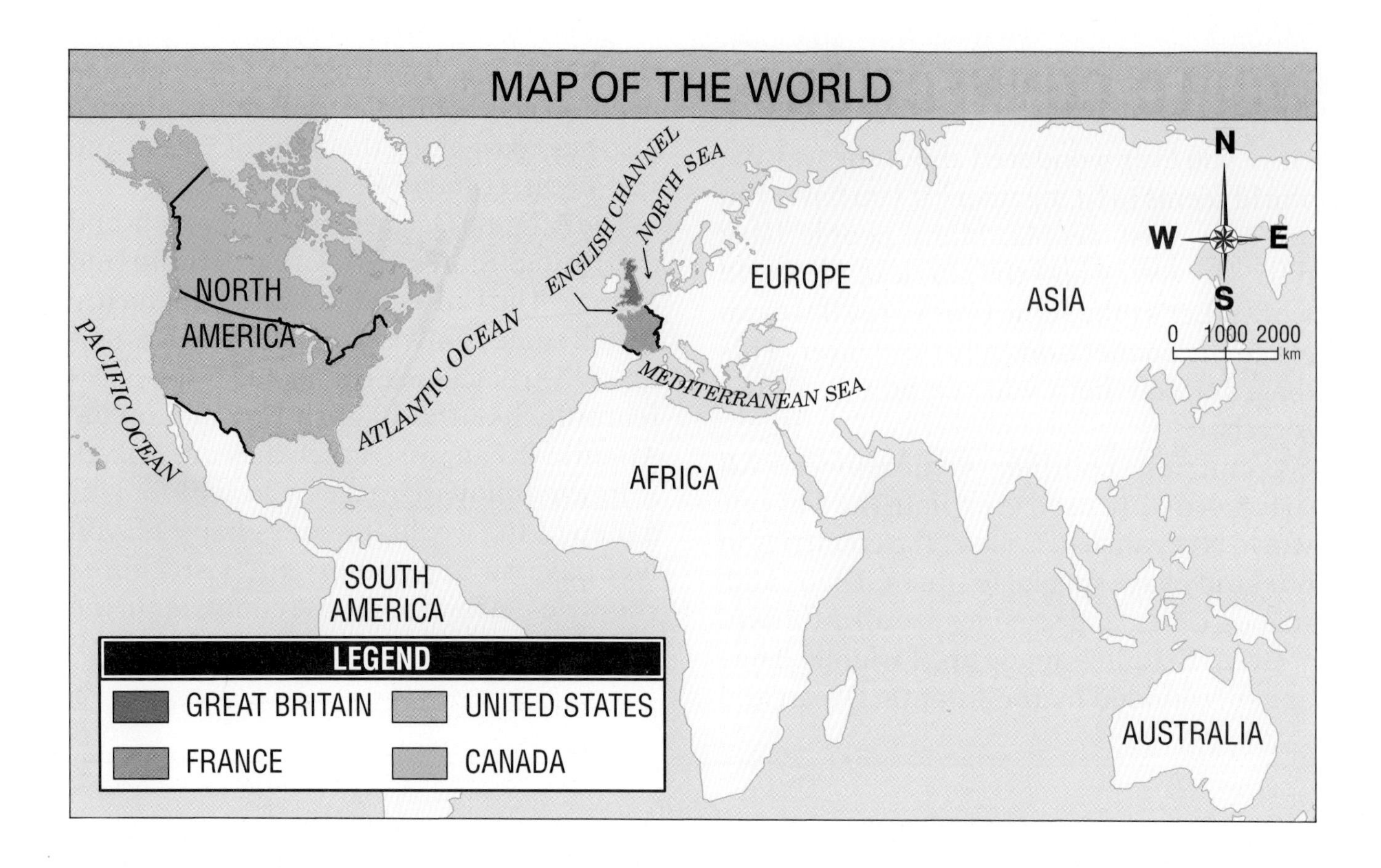

USING MAPS

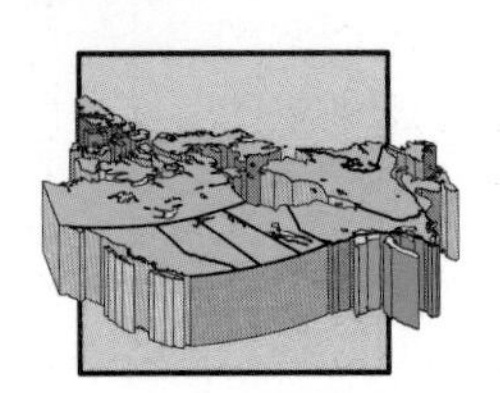

Three of the countries in our world that are linked with Canada are Great Britain, France, and the United States. Canada has been connected to these three countries for hundreds of years. The links began before Canada became a country. In the next chapter you will read more about the historical links between these countries. Right now, we will get started by using a map to help us locate them.

Different maps will give different kinds of information. The map on this page shows the world. Find the United States, Great Britain, and France on the map. Can you find all of the oceans we talked about earlier?

There are some features you can expect to find on most maps. These are symbols which help you understand maps.

Directional Symbol

North, South, East, and West are called **cardinal directions**. On a map they help us to know which way we are going when we travel places.

Directional symbols are shown in different ways on maps. Sometimes just the letters N, S, W, and E will be shown along the outside edges of the map. Which direction is Great Britain from Canada? Which direction is France from Canada? Which direction is the United States from Canada?

Legend

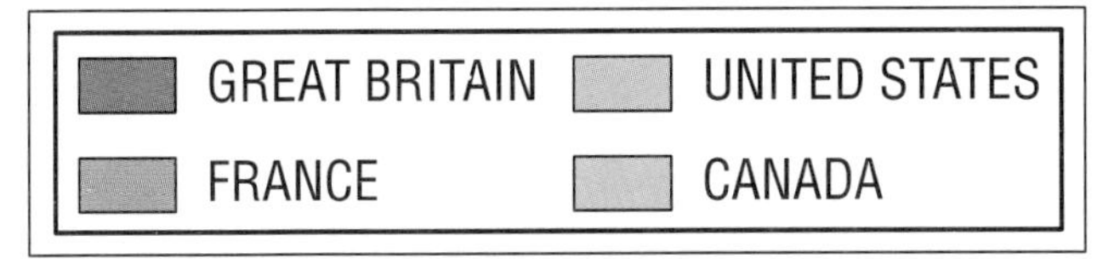

Legends use colours or symbols to help you understand what is happening on different parts of a map. Sometimes a map will use both colours and symbols. You can find this out by checking the legend as the first step in map reading.

Usually colours are used to show large areas. Symbols are used to show specific places or activities like forests or where you might expect to see farming taking place. How has colour been used on this map?

Scale

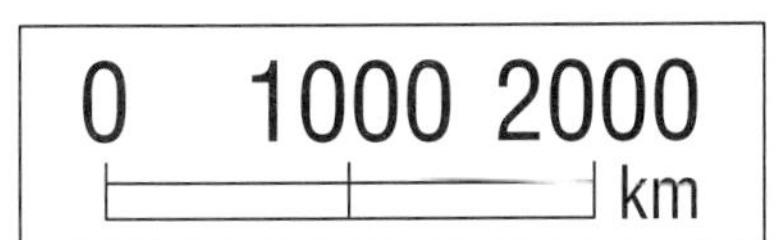

Maps are a way of showing something that is actually much bigger. A map will usually have a scale to help you calculate how far it actually is from place to place. On a scale, you will find a measure. Look at the scale on this map. You can use the scale to see how large a country is. How large is Canada? In which country could you travel from north to south in the shortest distance? How far is this distance?

MAP-MAKER'S TOOLBOX

This map-maker's toolbox will help you to prepare maps of your own. Make a map of Canada. This toolbox will tell you how.

Materials You Will Need

- ruler
- pencil crayons
- unlined paper

Planning

- decide the purpose of your map
- design your legend
- decide the size of map you will make
- decide if you will use a scale
- choose a title for your map

Hints

- draw first in pencil
- go over your outline with black
- put labels and symbols on before you colour
- use printing instead of handwriting
- shade lightly instead of colouring boldly
- use blue only to show water

1. **Name each province and territory.**
2. **Name the bodies of water—the oceans, lakes, and four major rivers.**
3. **Put a directional symbol on your map.**

The next six pages will give you some information about Britain, France, and the United States of America. Studying the pictures and information will help you imagine what each of these countries is like. Each page is called a potpourri because it gives you a mixture of information.

GREAT BRITAIN POTPOURRI

Capital City:
London, England
Official Language:
English
Area:
244 100 square km
Population:
57 293 000
Currency:
pound
Highest Mountain:
Ben Nevis, Scotland, 1343 m
Longest River:
Thames River, 340 km
Highest Building:
Canary Wharf Tower, 244 m
Important Airport:
Heathrow Airport, London, handles the largest amount of international traffic

Great Britain is made up of England, Scotland, Wales, and Northern Ireland. It has one government and one royal family.

FRANCE POTPOURRI

Capital City:
Paris
Official Language:
French
Area:
543 965 square km
Population:
56 236 000
Currency:
franc
Highest Mountain:
Mont Blanc, 4810 m
Longest River:
Loire, 1015 km
Important Landmarks:
Arc de Triomphe,
Eiffel Tower
Important Airport:
Charles de Gaulle, Paris

France is divided into 21 regions. Paris, the capital city of France, is visited every year by people from all over the world. They go to see the beautiful cathedrals, the Eiffel Tower, and museums like the Louvre.

THE UNITED STATES OF AMERICA POTPOURRI

Capital City:
Washington, D.C.

Official Language:
English

Area:
9 372 571 square km

Population:
250 372 000

Currency:
dollar

Highest Mountain:
Mount McKinley, Alaska, 6194 m

Longest River:
Mississippi-Missouri, 6020 km

Highest Building:
Sears Tower, Chicago, 443 m

Important Landmark:
Statue of Liberty, New York

Important Airport:
Chicago's O'Hare Field is the world's busiest

The United States of America is a very large country, and it is Canada's nearest neighbour. Like Canada, the United States has links with both France and England.

WAY OF LIFE

The potpourri pages showed images of each of the countries under study. What about the people who live in each country? How do they live? In this section you will read about how where you live affects the way you live.

Let's explore this section by asking three questions.

- Where do you live?
- What do you do in your spare time?
- What do you do to have fun?

You might go for a walk, read a book, watch tv, or play a game of baseball with your friends. Write down 10 things that you like to do for fun.

All of the activities you wrote down help to describe your **lifestyle**. What you do helps explain how you live. Now, add another bit of information to the equation: the weather. How does the weather affect what you do? Does the weather on each day help you decide what clothes you will wear?

Write down 10 things you like to do on hot, sunny days, on rainy days, and on cold, snowy days.

In this section of *Canadian Connections*, you have an opportunity to find out what kinds of things your classmates like to do. Read the **Surveyor's Toolbox**. Then you will be ready to do a survey.

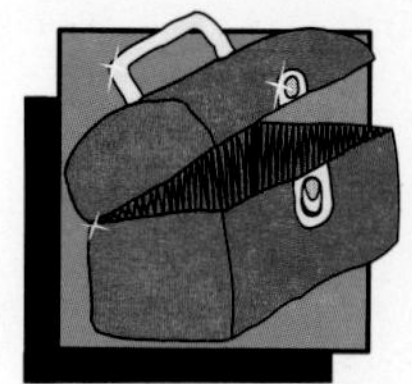

SURVEYOR'S TOOLBOX

A survey is like an interview. It allows you to collect information that would not be found in other types of reference books. A survey can be done in person or by sending it to the people to be surveyed. If you are doing your survey in person, follow the same guidelines you would use to prepare for an interview. An **Interviewer's Toolbox** can be found on page 43 of this book.

This toolbox will help you prepare a survey to send out.

Planning

- decide what you want to learn
- decide if you will use Yes/No, or Agree/Disagree answers, or if you want people to answer in their own words
- design the question sheet
- write a letter to the people who will get the survey, telling them who you are, what the survey is about, and how you will use the information

Sending Out the Survey

- send your survey and your letter at the same time
- tell when you want the survey back
- arrange a way for the survey to be returned

Use the images on this page to conduct your survey. Some of the questions you might ask are:

1. What sports do you play?
2. Have you ever eaten a crêpe?
3. When does your school have holidays? Do you know why?
4. What do you like to do for fun?

Have you ever been to a rodeo? The first rodeo was held in 1888 in the town of Prescott, Arizona. Many people who have never seen a rodeo dress in blue jeans or even cowboy boots and hats.

Have you ever eaten crêpes? The man in this picture is making crêpes. Crêpes are like very thin pancakes. They are often filled with fruit, seafood, or even chocolate.

Are you a member of the Girl Guides or Boy Scouts? Young people all over the world have joined these groups to have fun and to learn important skills.

USING THE INFORMATION

Sports
Food
Holidays
Music
Television

How are you influenced by these things?

By now you can probably tell that we are influenced by almost everything that goes on around us. We are influenced by our history, our family, and our friends, and by the things we see and do. It is the same for countries. This is because countries are made up of groups of people.

If you watch the news on television, listen to the radio news, or read newspapers and magazines, you can be influenced by what you read. Newspapers and magazines show how Canada is a neighbour to other countries in the world.

CANADA'S NEIGHBOURS

Canada has many neighbours in the world, and people have come here from all parts of the world to live. As people make their homes in this country, they tie Canada to other countries in the world.

Let's look at Josie's Cartoon Story to discover more about the meaning of three key terms.

Interaction *happens when people come together to talk, to do something together, or to share ideas.*

Links *are a kind of long-term interaction. They are formed when people share an interest, an idea, or a purpose.*

Influence *happens when we learn something new from someone else. It may be as simple as an idea we store in our mind. It may also cause us to change the way we think or the way we do something.*

PERSONAL JOURNAL

A personal journal is one way to make notes that will help you remember new things you have learned. It is also a place where you can write about feelings you have about something you have learned. You can ask yourself questions or make diagrams.

Some days you might just want to write down what you learned during class. Other times, you might respond to a question your teacher asks you or a question that you find in this book. You might even ask yourself a question and try to work out an answer as you write! The most important thing is that you use your journal to help yourself understand what you have learned.

a. You may have a friend who has moved to Canada from another part of the world. From what you know, make your own cartoon story about your friend. Be sure to include ways that your friend is an example of interaction, links, and influence. If you need help, look back to Josie's Cartoon Story.

b. In your school library, locate the reference section. Ask the librarian to help you find the large thesaurus. A thesaurus is a book that shows synonyms and antonyms. Look up the new terms you've learned: interaction, links, and influence. Beside each term, list any synonyms you find in the thesaurus.

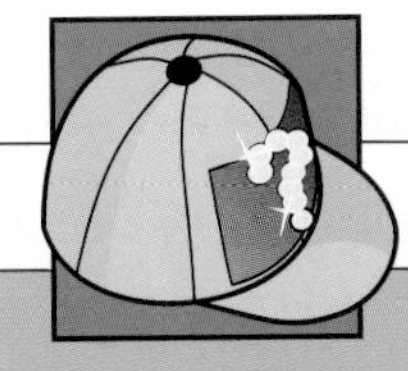

THINKING CAP

Brainstorming is a way to collect as many ideas as possible about a topic. Sometimes, by hearing the ideas other people have, you will be able to make connections and come up with new ideas.

Brainstorming works best if you follow some simple rules. They are

- accept and record every idea
- record ideas in the words of the speaker
- allow everyone a chance
- don't repeat ideas
- no put-downs

a. Try brainstorming one of these topics:
   - Potpourri Canada
   - Ways the world has influenced your community
   - Ways Canada is linked to other countries

b. Begin a class web to show how Canada is linked to other countries. Each time you discover a new connection, add it to your web. The web shown here is a beginning. Can you see how the ideas are organized to show how they are connected? Can you add to the web using what you learned in the last two chapters?

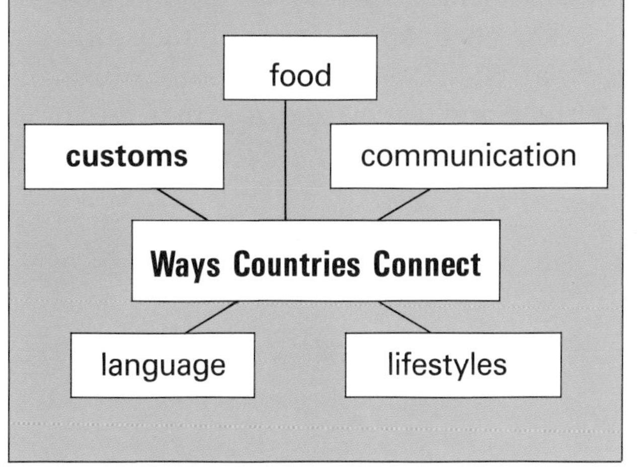

CHAPTER WRAP-UP

Maps are an important tool that we use to see how the Earth looks. From maps we can get an idea about where places are located, physical features, and information about distance and size.

In this chapter, we focused on the locations of Canada, the United States, Britain, and France. On our map we can see that one of Canada's world neighbours, the United States, shares the North American continent with us. We can see that the Atlantic Ocean separates Canada and the United States from Britain and France. Britain and France are located in Europe.

For hundreds of years, the distance between the North American continent and Europe kept travelers from meeting each other. Because motorized vehicles had not yet been invented, exploring other lands took an enormous amount of time. Until Europeans landed on the shores of North America, there had only been rumours and legends that told of distant lands on the other side of the Atlantic. As you will discover in the next chapter, Native people also had legends that **predicted** the coming of white people. When these people from different parts of the world finally met, their interaction strongly influenced how Canada's future would develop.

In the next chapter, we will take a closer look at what happened when the French, English, and Native **cultures** met, and how they influenced each other.

Do you remember the questions you learned to ask from the **Surveyor's Toolbox** and from the **Interviewer's Toolbox**? They were designed to help you learn more about yourself and others, and to help you examine different lifestyles. Keep these types of questions in mind while we explore the connections between Canadian, American, British, and French people, and the influences they have on each other.

ACTIVITIES

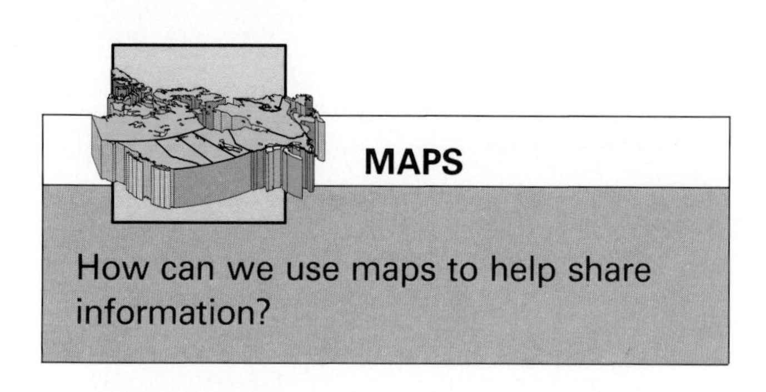

How can we use maps to help share information?

Put your survey in your personal journal.

DESIGN YOUR OWN ICON

Design an icon that can be used whenever Canada's links are studied. In this chapter, you had the chance to study the potpourri pages of Great Britain, France, and the United States. The **Surveyor's Toolbox** and the **Interviewer's Toolbox** showed you how to collect information. Now create your own potpourri page for Canada. Be sure to include your new icon on the potpourri page.

CHAPTER

2

CANADA'S TIES TO THE PAST

PREVIEW PAGE

In this chapter, you will go back in time. You will read stories about what it was like to live in early Canada. You will see how French and British ways of living were used in Canada. We will explore how the fight between France and Britain affected where people chose to settle. For example, the French and the British fished off the same coast. They each set up territories for their fishing stations. The British concentrated mainly in the eastern Avalon Peninsula in present day Newfoundland. The French had scattered stations along the coast and on Cape Breton. We will look at how Natives fared in this division of land and power.

EXPLORATION AND SETTLEMENT

Hundreds of years before Europeans came to North America, Native people had settled in Canada. It is believed that these people came to North America across a land bridge between the Soviet Union and Alaska.

There is evidence that Norse people sailed from Iceland and Greenland down the eastern coast of Canada around 1000 AD and made a temporary settlement in northern Newfoundland at L'Anse aux Meadows. Song-stories about Leif the Lucky, son of Eric the Red, tell of him naming Markland and Vinland, the land he found.

Historians think this land was probably in southern Labrador and the Cape Cod region. People will never really know why the Norse people didn't remain in North America. Some stories say that Native people eventually chased them away. Other stories say that some of the Norse people stayed in Canada and lived with Natives.

In Europe, there were only rumours of mysterious lands. The rumours hinted that another world might exist beyond the Atlantic Ocean. Some told of the Spanish finding gold and strange people. Natives had similar legends that predicted the coming of white people from across the Great Waters.

In 1497, John Cabot sailed from England on a ship named *Matthew*. He was trying to find another passage to *Cipango*, or Japan. Instead, he came upon the great fishing banks of Canada. In 1534, Jacques Cartier, a French explorer, reached the Gulf of St. Lawrence and claimed the region for France.

Canada's **first peoples** *often used dog sleds in winter. The Natives lived in harmony with the land and animals. When Europeans came, the Natives taught them how to live in Canada.*

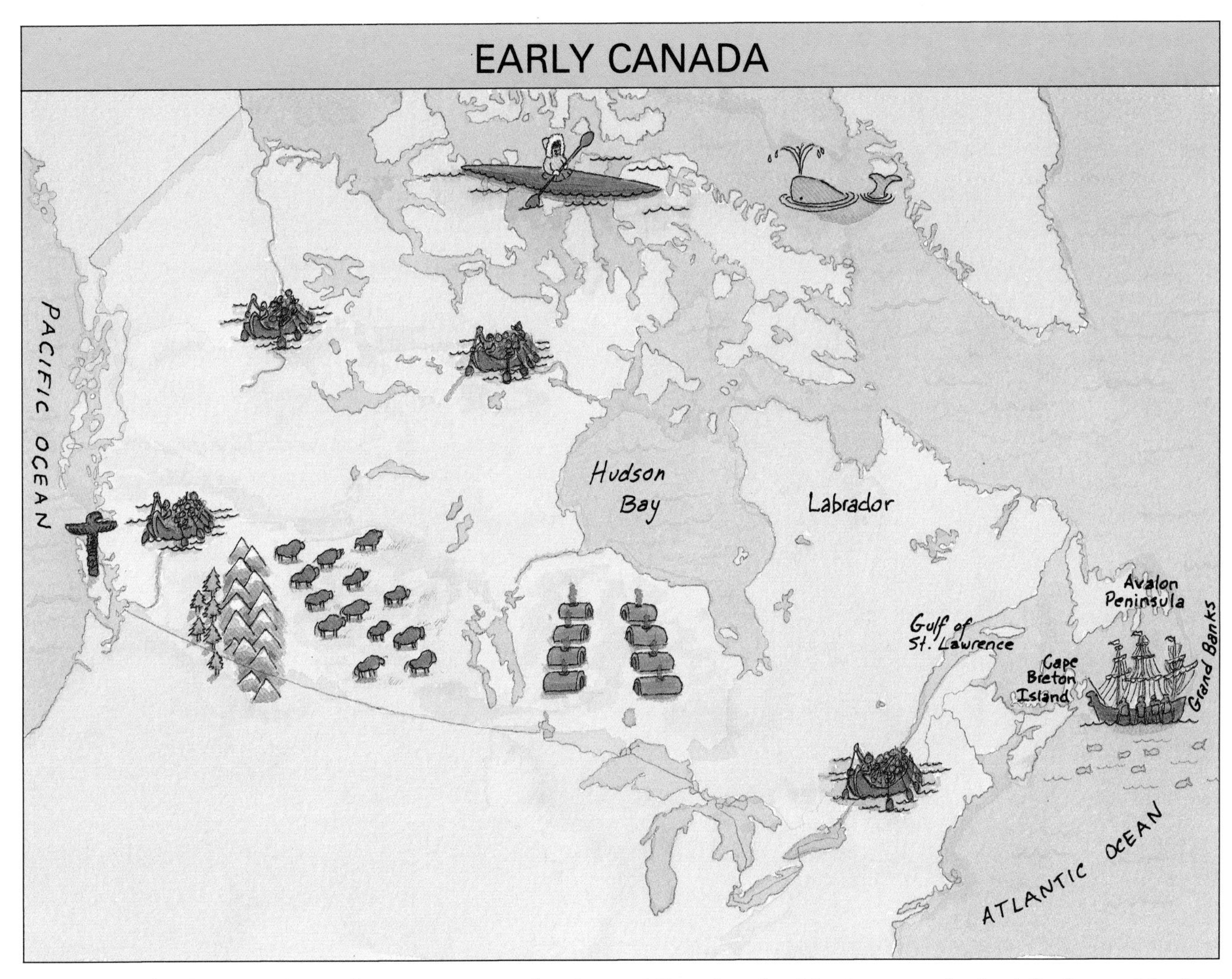

When the first sailing ships came to the Grand Banks, the Natives traded with them. Native people had villages throughout Canada. The coureur de bois learned to use the rivers as the Natives did.

France and Britain were competing to claim new lands. When they discovered Canada's rich fish and fur resources, the fight was on. They both tried to control the land and the resources.

The French and British had a kind of partnership with Native groups. Without the help of Native people, neither the French nor the British would have lived through the first winter. Native people acted as guides, teachers, and sometimes as close friends to these new people.

MAPS

1. In your notebook, give a name for each illustration on the map.
2. Find the Avalon Peninsula.
3. Why do you think waterways were so important in history?
4. Find the Grand Banks.

We will begin our journey into the past by reading a story about a 10-year-old British boy named Timothy Stuart. One type of journal is called a diary. In a diary, the writer keeps a record of the important events of each day. This is Timothy's diary telling about his journey to Canada on a fishing ship.

FISHING

Day 1: *Well, this is June, the year is 1668, and me mum is pretty sad to see me leaving on a fishing ship to this new world. An old fisherman told me the place I'm going to is called Canada. It's supposed to be named after a Native word meaning a group of huts. Another fellow overheard us talking and said, "No, it's from the Cree word* Kanata, *meaning a fresh clean land." Anyway, I'm going to be a cabin boy. I'll help with the cooking and the cleaning up, and I'll learn to be a fisherman. Times are hard for me family what with me dad being dead and me poor mum with six mouths to feed—so I thinks it's best that I be making my own way. The ship I'm going on is called* Flying Sprite. *She's a clean-looking rig with three masts.*

Day 30: *We have enough rations to do us until we arrive. It's crowded on the ship. Some of the men have been sick, but no one has died yet. I'm told we're the lucky ones. Some ships have arrived with the men full of* **disease** *and half starving. This voyage takes from anywhere to 42 to 65 days to complete, depending on the weather and the type of ship.*

Day 62: *We finally arrived at a place called Grand Banks, off the coast of Newfoundland. The fish are so plentiful you could scoop them up with a shovel. There's lots of work to do. After we catch the fish we will go ashore. There are huts and store houses built there. And drying racks, or* flacks *as some of the men call them. Fishers used to just salt the fish and bring them back to Britain* **green**. *Too many of them spoiled. Now what with us drying them first, not so many of them rot on the way back home. I've been told some Micmac Natives will be on shore. They like to trade furs for some of our goods like axes and blankets. Imagine, me going back home with furs and knowing how to fish for me keep!*

DESIGN YOUR OWN ICON

1. Based on Timothy's story, draw pictures of what he described. You could draw a ship's captain, or a scene with people trading or fishing.

SETTLEMENT PATTERNS

For almost 100 years, the fishers traded with the Natives who came to the coast with furs. The Natives traded for guns, pails, knives, and other European goods. Many of the European goods made the life of the Natives easier. The Europeans took the furs home and made a great deal of money. Europeans found the furs to be **fashionable**.

Natives traded with Europeans for many items. Name some of the items in this photograph that the Natives would have received from the Europeans.

This is a beaver. Felt hats made from beaver fur were fashionable in Great Britain.

The land area where most of this trading occurred included present-day New Brunswick, Nova Scotia, and part of the state of Maine. The area became known as Acadia. With so much wealth to be had from the land and sea, a group of Frenchmen decided to try to control all of the trade in Acadia. In the early 1600s, they set up a trading post. The post, at Port Royal, did not last without women and children. Family life was needed to make the settlement permanent. It wasn't until the 1630s that permanent settlement in Acadia took place.

The French had another area of settlement in present-day province of Quebec. Samuel de Champlain founded New France. Settlements grew at Montreal, Quebec City, and along the shores between the two.

At the same time that the French were settling New France, the British were establishing their territory around the Hudson Bay and along the eastern seaboard, south of Acadia. The British called their settlements the Thirteen Colonies. As the competition between the countries grew more intense, Natives began to pick sides. For example, the Huron became French **allies**, while the Iroquois sided with the British.

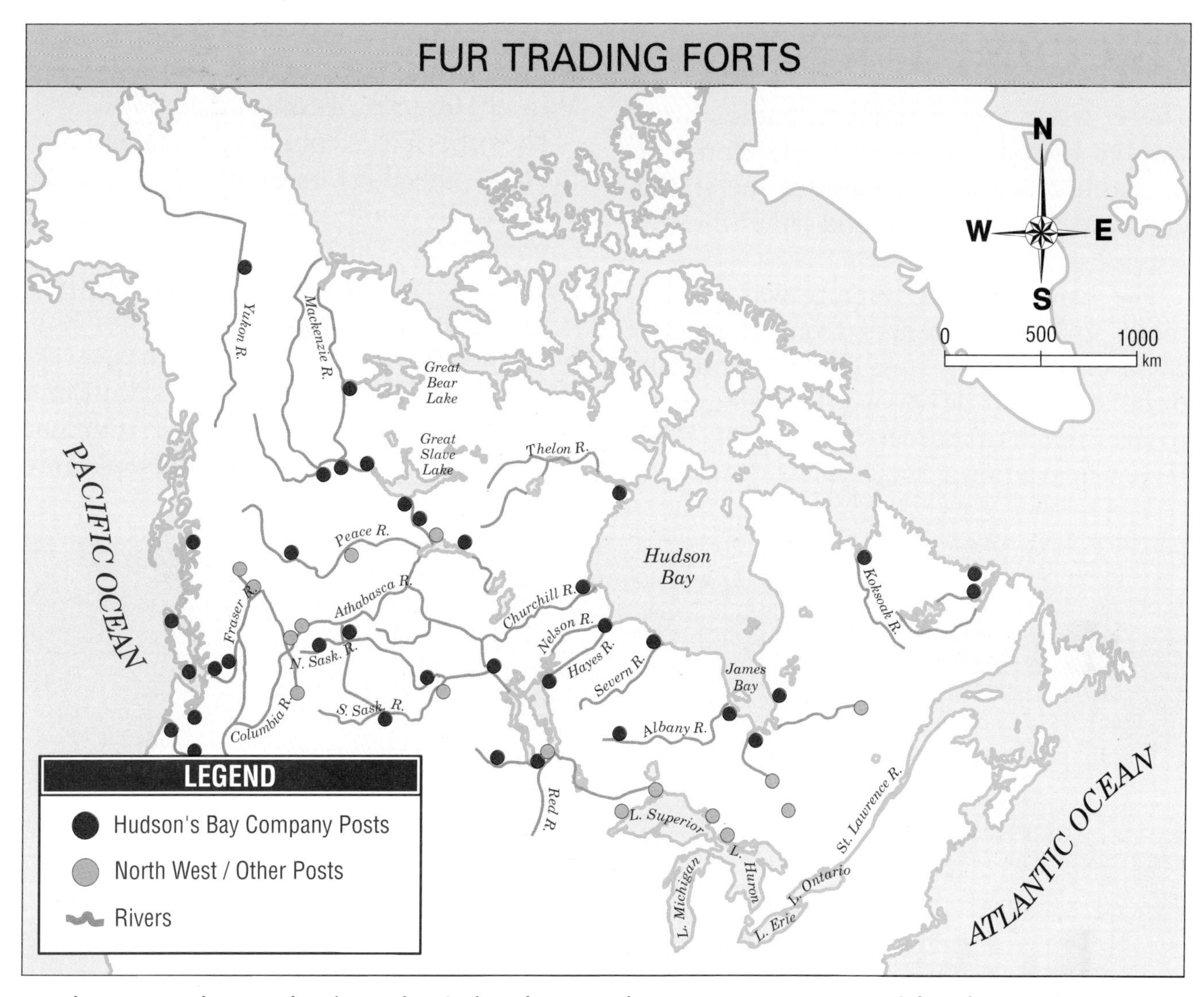

This map shows the forts built by the North West Company and by the Hudson's Bay Company.

Both the French and the British were serious about getting control of the land and the fur trade. They looked for new sources of furs. The rivers **enabled** them to travel further into the new land. Some of the Native peoples helped too. They became **middlemen**. As middlemen they traveled the river inland to collect furs from other Natives. Then, they brought the furs back to the traders.

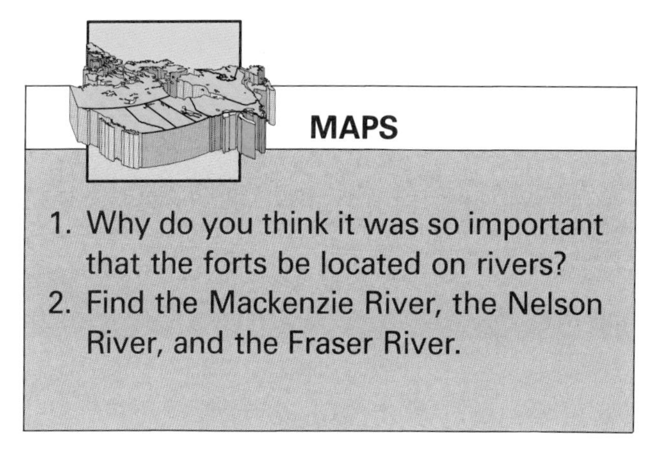

MAPS

1. Why do you think it was so important that the forts be located on rivers?
2. Find the Mackenzie River, the Nelson River, and the Fraser River.

FUR COMPANIES

There were two main companies who wanted to control the fur trade. You will probably recognize the name of one. In the end, one company won and ruled the fur trade.

The North West Company was mostly made up of fur traders from Montreal. Some of the Nor'Westers had been coureur de bois. Coureur de bois was the name given to the French fur traders who traveled the rivers to trade for furs. These men were mostly farmers who did their trading in the winter. In the next section, you will meet Marcel Monteux, a coureur de bois.

The other large company was known as the Hudson's Bay Company. This company was run by traders who had come from Great Britain. The Hudson's Bay Company also wanted to control the fur trade. At first, it only built forts near the Hudson Bay. Soon the traders realized they must go west if they were to win. The Hudson's Bay Company built forts along the great rivers that went west. In the end, the Hudson's Bay

Fort Garry was a Hudson's Bay Company **factory** *on the Red River. The Red River carts lined up outside of the fort were built by Metis people.*

Company was more successful than the North West Company. The Hudson's Bay Company controlled the fur trade.

Finding new sources of furs was important. This meant exploring new lands. Both companies did a lot of exploring. People were sent to explore west along the river routes. Alexander Mackenzie, David Thompson, and Simon Fraser were three of the men who went exploring. Three of the rivers they traveled were named after them.

REPORT WRITING

1. Write a report on one of the following explorers:
   Alexander Mackenzie
   David Thompson
   Simon Fraser
   Include information about how the Native people helped the explorer.

REPORT WRITER'S TOOLBOX

Planning

- identify key questions to be answered or prepare an outline
- decide where you can go to get information
- make a work schedule showing research days and writing days

Researching

- use a variety of resources (for example, printed material, maps, pictures, tapes, or film)
- use your own words
- never use words you don't understand
- select information that seems accurate
- do not use fiction or one person's **opinion**

Organizing and Sorting

- use your outline or research questions to help put your information in order
- make sure it still makes the best sense to use that order
- if you have pieces of information saying opposite things, look for another source or decide if it may be better not to use the information
- decide where to include maps, charts, or illustrations

Writing

- decide if you are going to write out your report or use the computer
- design a title page that includes your full name, the date, and a title for your work
- introduce your report so that a reader knows what you are going to write about
- change paragraphs with each new main idea
- leave space for visuals or do them as you go
- include a conclusion that reviews the main points you have made (Hint: The conclusion is often much like the introduction. It is also a good place to tell your opinion about what you have learned.)

P.S. Show you care—do it neatly!

To get a personal picture of what it was like to be part of Canada's fur industry, read the following story about Marcel Monteux.

COUREUR DE BOIS

"Bonjour, I am Marcel Monteux. I am what you call a coureur de bois... heh... en anglais... a runner of the woods. I am an agent for some Montreal fur traders. I run with the Natives. They teach me to snowshoe, canoe, and hunt. We get the fur for the merchants and they supply us with goods that we cannot get in the woods—like guns, blankets, whiskey, and axes. There is great opportunity here in this new land.

"I left France when I was 14. Here in Canada, it is the same, but it is different. You are thinking that I speak in riddles? Here the Natives are friendly with some Natives, but not friendly with some others, just like people in France. Here people want a better life, just like in France. We bring our customs, religion, and language here, but we also must adjust to a land full of trees and waters, no big churches or roads, no **operas** *or fancy carriages. But Natives have songs and dancing here, their own rights and wrongs, and great freedom to roam. The Natives know how to live with this land.*

"I am thinking that when you take away the customs and the clothes—people are just people... Marcel the great thinker, non. But I also worry, you know. I live with a Native woman. We have a baby together. And I am noticing that the merchants aren't after anything except fur, fur, fur! What do you suppose will happen to my family and me when they don't want fur anymore?"

In the next section you will read about some of the things that the French brought with them to set up New France. Their ideas and ways of doing things continue to be a lively part of Canada today.

The coureur de bois lived and worked in the wilderness. Marcel Monteux worked, canoed, traded, and trapped. The fur trade was his **livelihood**.

A CHANGING LIFESTYLE

Before the traders and settlers came, North America had been home only to Native people. They had explored and lived on the lands from the coldest regions of the north to the great grassy plains of the south. Some Natives were farmers, others were hunters. Some had permanent villages, others moved their homes in search of food.

Life changed forever for the Native people when the Europeans arrived. Some of the changes would be seen as good. Others would not. Many of the Native people died of the European diseases like cholera. Some of the Natives married Europeans. The children that the Native women had with European men were called **Metis**. The lives of these children would be influenced by the beliefs and customs of both their parents' cultures.

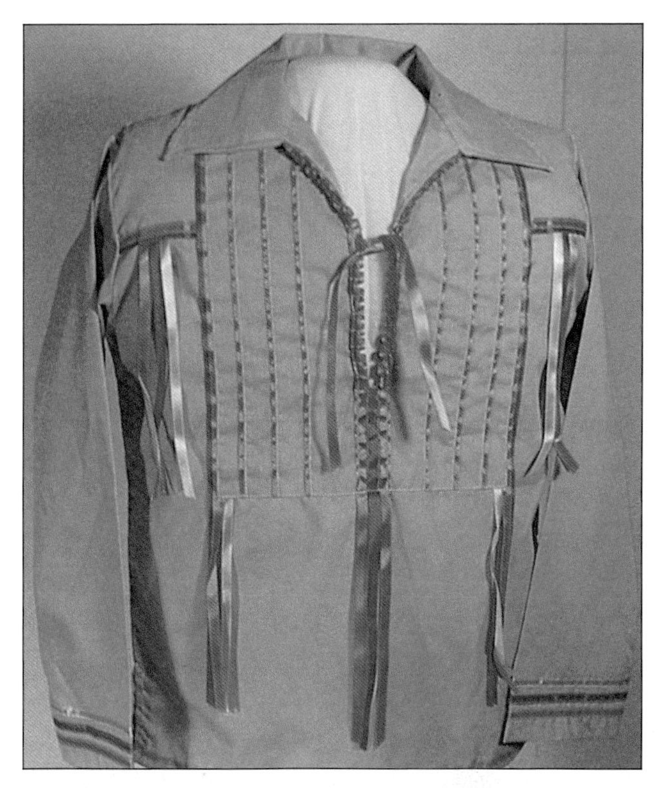

Metis clothing was a blend of European tailoring and Native materials. Their clothing was colourful and practical.

LINKS OF CULTURE

We know that settlements formed when people came to the east coast of North America. The settlers who came from France formed their own communities. The settlers who came from Britain also formed their own communities. There were also many Native communities that had been in the area for hundreds of years. The Native people had their own languages. They had their own religion. They also had a style of building that they used to make their homes. The Metis used the technology of all three cultures to make their homes.

When the British and French settlements began, they were not like those of the Natives. Although the settlers' communities were different from those in their homelands, they were similar in other ways. The settlers used the language of their homeland to communicate with each other. They kept the same religion that they had had in their homeland. The **architecture** of the buildings they built was similar to buildings in their homeland.

When the British and French came to North America, they came with a knowledge about technology used in their homelands. The Native people also had a knowledge about the technology they used in their lifestyle. Language, beliefs, and architecture are all parts of culture. In chapters 5 and 6, you will read more about beliefs and language. The following pages will show the British and French influences on the way land was settled.

All along the St. Lawrence River, seigneuries were used. This painting shows Château Richer, about 25 km northeast of Quebec City.

PLACE-ROYALE AT QUEBEC CITY

This settlement, Place-Royale, is sometimes called the birthplace of Quebec City. It is located on the shores of the St. Lawrence River. This is where Champlain built a small fort in 1608. The fort was a place to store furs and other goods. It was also a living place for himself and his men. As traders and settlers came, more buildings were constructed. Place-Royale is said to be one of the first important French settlements in Canada.

What was it like to be a settler in early Canada? Imagine yourself on the St. Lawrence River in about 1702. It's a warm summer day. You can see the shimmering blue waters of the river, and on either side of the banks are sturdy whitewashed houses built of stone. They are similar to the houses that were built in France. They are long and low to the ground, with steeply pitched roofs that have massive chimneys on the ends.

You should notice that the **cultivated** land behind the houses runs in long narrow strips. That is because travel by land is difficult and sometimes dangerous, so the farmers build close to the river and treat it like a great highway. There's a big house that sits near the smaller homes. It's the manor of the seigneur. He owns the land the farmers work. They give the seigneur rent money because he lets them make a living off his property.

The farmers grow peas, barley, rye, and corn. They may have a few cows, some chickens, and maybe even a small tobacco patch.

Life is not all work for these early settlers. In the evening they may sit by their **hearths** and sing folk songs. Winter is especially full with singing, dancing, playing the fiddle, and celebrating festivals such as St. Martin's Day on November 11.

BRITISH CONTROL

By 1715, the English control of lands in the **New World** was growing. Acadia was now under British rule. In 1759, the English also captured New France.

In the early years of settlement, Britain had allowed the colonies to make many decisions about their lifestyles. In many ways, the colonists maintained links with Britain. Ships traveled back and forth between the colonies and Britain and there was a steady trade of fish and furs. The colonists kept the language, the religion, and many of the customs of their old life in Britain.

The colonists worked hard to make a good life for themselves. They were proud of their successes in their new homeland. Many of the colonies had established their own governments. Some of the people were beginning to feel that the colonies were strong and able to stand on their own. Once Britain had control of all the lands in the New World, the British government wanted to be in charge of its colonies. This did not please many of the colonists. They did not think it was fair that a government so far away should make decisions about their lives. Other colonists believed that they should remain loyal to the king of England and the government of Britain. These people called themselves the **Loyalists**.

Thousands of Loyalists moved to Canada from the American colonies. They wanted to remain loyal to England and could not do so if they stayed where they were.

DIFFERENT POINTS OF VIEW

Most people have **beliefs** about how their lives should be run. Not everyone has the same beliefs. When people have different beliefs, they will sometimes disagree. Having disagreements is normal. When disagreements happen, people need to take time to know the different points of view before they decide how to act on the disagreement. Here are three different points of view about who should be in charge of the English colonies in the New World.

Some people, like Thomas Ross, did not believe that England should have control of America.

"My name is Thomas Ross. I came to the colonies 30 years ago. I have built a successful printing business in Boston. When I was a young man, I fought in the English troops of the colony. I helped to make this colony strong. King George now wants control over something he has not been a part of. His government makes decisions about our lives. We are not able to have a colonist as a member of that government. Who hears our voices? Is this fair that someone who does not know our lives is able to make decisions about them? I am frustrated. Last month, we were told we must pay taxes to England on goods we bring in by ship for our use. I do not object to paying a tax, but I think it should go to our government here, not to the government in England. The colonies must break away from England and make their own decisions. It is time for ***self-government****."*

The king of England wanted all of the colonists to remain loyal to England.

"I am George III, king of England. Without the support of the British government, the New World would never have grown strong. It was Britain who paid for the exploration that found the New World. It was Britain who sent troops to protect you in the battles for the lands to the

north. Without the money and support of Britain, the colonies would never have been established. The colonies are making money. As part of our **empire**, *you should be proud to support your homeland. Your loyalty will be rewarded with our wisdom and our protection. We are your family."*

Some people, like Samuel Booth, chose to remain loyal to England. They had to move to Canada where people still respected England.

"Samuel Booth is my name. I am an Englishman who lives outside New York. In England, my family was poor. Our land was not large enough to support a family. The opportunity to come to the colonies meant I would be able to have a better life. Here, I feel safe and I can still be an Englishman. I grew up respecting the power of the **monarchy**. *The monarchy is what has made Britain strong. The colonies need the strength of the monarchy. I will not turn my back on the country of my birth. I will not turn my back on my king. I must remain loyal because I know that Britain will always do what is best for us."*

SOLVING THE PROBLEM

Disagreements like this one can be solved in a number of ways. Taking time to know the other points of view is an important first step. When people are able to see the problem in different ways, they are often able to find a solution they can agree upon. In history, these groups of people were not successful in using talk to solve their disagreement.

The colonists who wanted to have their own government began a **revolution** against Britain. They refused to pay the taxes. They vandalized the ships that came from England. Life in the colonies became unpleasant for Loyalists. When a war broke out, some Loyalists chose not to fight for either side. Other Loyalists joined the British troops.

When the war ended, the colonists who wanted self-government had won. They were **independent** from Britain. Loyalists who had fought for Britain were told they could no longer live in the colonies of the new United States. Many of the Loyalists who left the United States moved to the British lands to the north. They settled in the areas that would later become parts of Canada.

Following the American Revolution (1775-1783), the United States split from Britain. The Treaty of Paris in 1783 formally recognized the United States of America. The movement of approximately 40 000 Loyalists into Nova Scotia and Quebec contributed to the different ways that the countries of Canada and the United States would develop.

Once the United States was recognized as a separate country from Britain, there were disagreements with Canada over **boundaries**.

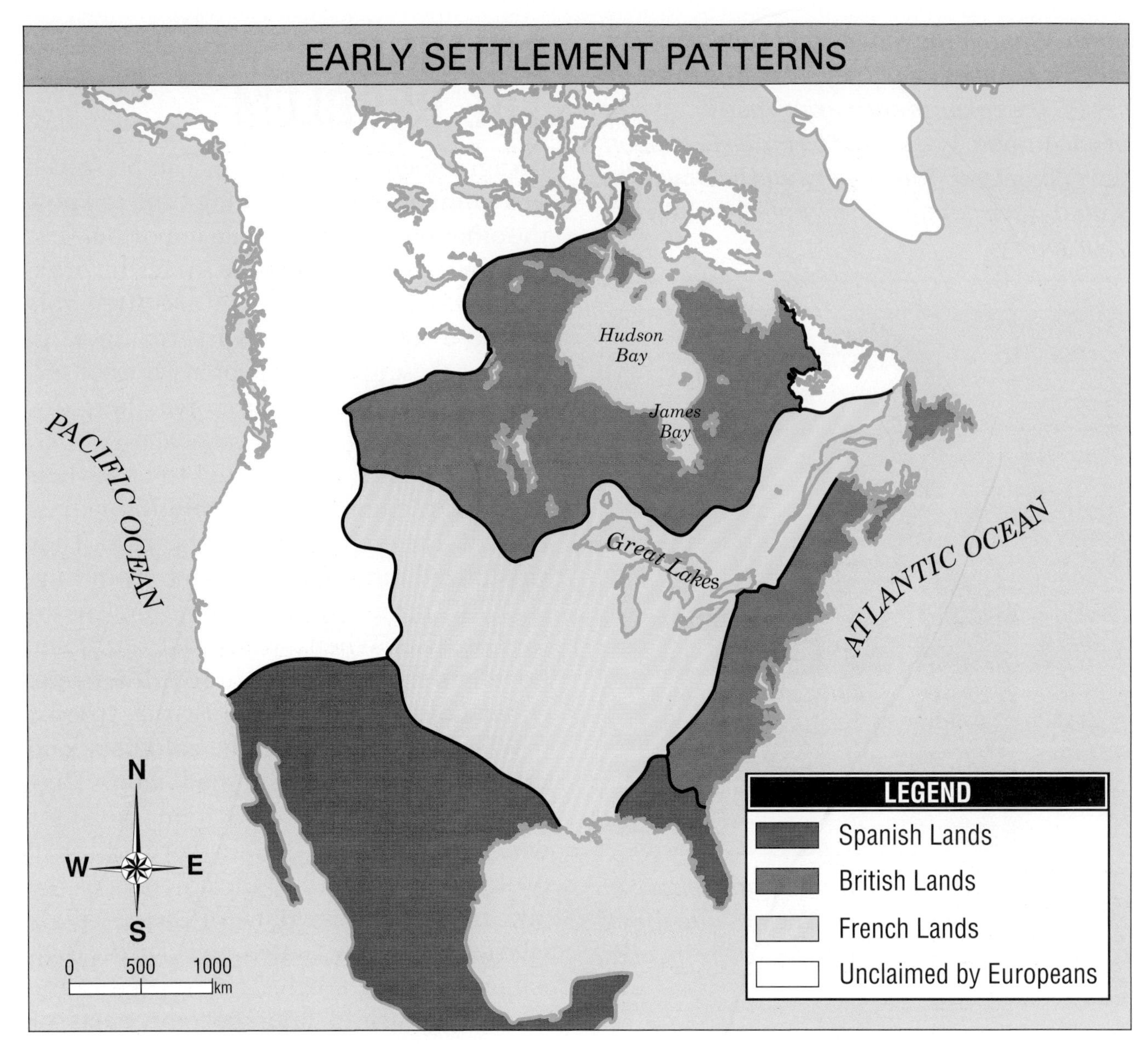

Britain and France, along with Spain, controlled most of the land in North America.

HISTORY UPDATE

Although many early settlers to the United States can trace their family roots back to Britain and France, their country did not keep up its **ties** to the old countries the way that Canada did. As you read in the previous section, the United States gained recognition as a country much earlier than Canada. Canada did not become the Dominion of Canada until 1867. Britain did not give

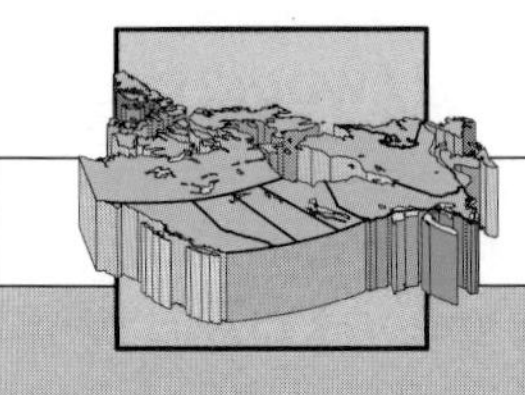

MAPS

1. Look at the lands claimed by the British and by the French. Where did Canada's Native people fit in?

Canada full control (**patriation**) until 1982. The queen of England is still recognized as a symbol of state in Canada.

Over time, Canada's relationship with Natives changed. As explained in this chapter, because of the fur trade, new Canadians and Natives had an **interdependent relationship**. While the fur trade lasted, many of the Natives worked alongside of the Europeans. When the fur trade declined, settlement became the main focus of Europeans. This change of view made the Natives less important to the Europeans. Agreements called **treaties** were made with Natives. Areas called **reserves** were set aside for them. Natives no longer had total control over where or how they lived.

Early settlement patterns were different between Canada and the United States. Canada was slower to settle its lands. Law and order were generally established by the North-West Mounted Police when settlers came to Western Canada.

In the United States, the settling of the West was marked by fierce battles between Natives and settlers. Canada had its share of disputes with Native and Metis groups, such as the **Riel Rebellion**, but Canada did not experience the extensive wars that occurred in the United States.

Once boundaries were settled and some time had passed, Canada and the United States became friendly neighbours.

The twentieth century was a turning point in developing better relationships between France, Britain, the United States, and Canada. All four countries were allies in the First World War (1914–1918) and in the Second World War (1939–1945). They are members of the **North Atlantic Treaty Organization** and were invaluable contributors to the creation of the United Nations. You will read more about international partnerships in chapter 6.

CHAPTER WRAP-UP

In this chapter you read about early travelers to Canada. Transportation is important to the linking of people and places. When people are able to move from one place to another, they are able to trade. Because North America had fish and furs, ships were sent to trade. This linked the people of Great Britain and France to North America. The coming of the Europeans changed the lives of the Native people.

Many Canadians and Americans can trace **ancestors** back to Britain and to France. Settlers to Canada and the United States brought their customs, languages, and religions to the New World.

In the next chapter, you will meet some Canadians. All of the people you will meet have some connection to the countries we are studying. Think about the way that they live. Is it similar to the way you live? What kinds of questions would you ask them if you were to interview them?

ACTIVITIES

EDITORIAL

Forming opinions is a challenging task. It is a responsible way of showing what we know and how we feel about what we know. A real opinion always has an answer to the question, "Why?" We can change our opinions as we learn new information. Changing your opinion when you have new information is also responsible.

Forming an opinion takes several steps. They are:

a) Understanding what the question or problem is asking.
b) Knowing some facts about what is happening.
c) Identifying everyone who might be involved.
d) Finding out the different points of view.
e) Deciding which point of view has the most in common with what you believe to be right.
f) Being ready to listen to others and to share your ideas.

Are you ready to take on the challenge? Go back into the chapter and select one of the influences shown. Follow through the first five steps. Find the other people in the class who selected the same influence that you selected. Meet in a group and have a discussion in which you share your opinions. Don't forget the listen part of the last step!

DESIGN YOUR OWN ICON

Write about how you feel about the fur trade in North America. Design a poster to show how you feel.

PERSONAL JOURNAL

In your journal, write what you think about the early settlers keeping their own culture. Take on the point of view of a Native person. Do you think that keeping the British or the French culture is a good idea or a poor idea? What do you feel? Why?

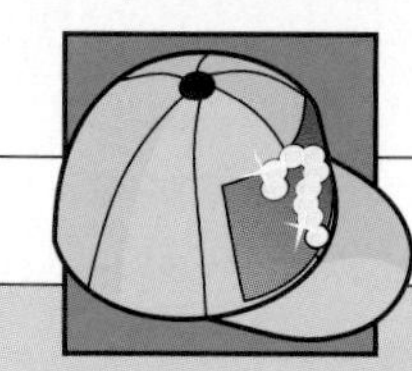

THINKING CAP

The French and the British had disagreements with each other before they came to Canada. They continued to fight with each other while Canada was being settled. Now that Canada is considered one country, do you see how past influences, links, and interactions are still affecting present-day Canada?

REPORT WRITING

Reports bring together **factual** information. Reports may contain maps, diagrams, and illustrations. Reports use a special style of language. Write a report on the fur trade. Use the following research questions to help you find the information you need.

a) Where did the fur trade take place? Where did the furs go?
   - Map
b) What furs were traded? How were the different furs used?
c) Who traded the furs? What was traded to get the furs?
   - Diagram or Chart
d) Why was the fur trade important in Canada's history?

CHAPTER

3

CANADA—THROUGH THE EYES OF OTHERS

PREVIEW PAGE

In the last chapter we looked at the formation of Canada and the United States. Canada and the United States have a shared history. Both nations grew up right next to each other. Because both countries had many settlers from Britain, the two countries are alike in many ways. Even so, they are also **unique**.

Unlike the United States, however, Canada was influenced by another **Old World** country—France. Spain and France were involved in the United States's early development, but they lost control. The French influence in Canada is still felt today. Unlike the other three countries being studied in this book, only Canada has two official languages.

In this chapter, you will have the opportunity to see Canada through the eyes of four young people. As you read about the lives of these four people, think about what it means to be Canadian. Is there something that makes Canadians completely different from American, French, and British people? For example, can you think of a special type of meal that **originated** in Canada? Also, as you read, think about the things you might have in common with our guests: Marilyn, Stanislas, Ralph, and Wanda.

MEET MARILYN CAMPBELL

"Hi! My name is Marilyn Campbell. Some people believe my ancestors were the first people to come to Canada. That was thousands of years ago when there was still a land bridge between North America and Eurasia. The land bridge was called Beringia. My ancestors came and settled in North America. My people chose to live on the West Coast. Today I live on Vancouver Island. I speak both the English language and Nootka. My people are called Nuu-Chah-Nulth, *which means 'All Along the Mountains.'*

"We have a good life living on this beautiful island. I am learning how to make a cedar canoe. I have always enjoyed launching our great canoe into the ocean with my mother and father and going to visit our relatives up the island. We have a car too! Going up the coast by canoe is just more fun sometimes, and more practical, too!

"My aunt is a fabulous cook. She shows me how to cook salmon and halibut. My mom's favourite meal is venison, *or deer meat. I know that my ancestors celebrated good hunting and fishing with festive meals. Sometimes they held* ***potlatches****. These were dinners where gifts were given to everyone who attended. Today we still have potlatches. I love to go. Everybody gets dressed up in their finest clothes. Long ago, that would have meant wearing clothing woven out of cedar bark. Today I wear modern clothes, and they are special.*

"This photograph shows one of my ancestors. Notice his cedar bark clothing."

"Many Inuit and North American Native groups have a long and proud tradition of storytelling and of creating beautiful chants. One of Canada's most famous poets is Pauline Johnson. Her father was a Mohawk chief, her mother was a British lady. Although Pauline was Metis, she considered herself a Native, and celebrated her Mohawk heritage. I would like to share one of her beautiful poems with you."

The Lost Lagoon

It is dusk on the Lost **Lagoon**,
And we two dreaming the dusk away,
Beneath the drift of a twilight grey,
Beneath the drowse of an ending day,
And the curve of a golden moon.

It is dark in the Lost Lagoon,
And gone are the depths of the haunting blue,
The grouping gulls, and the old canoe,
The singing firs, and the dusk and—you,
And gone is the golden moon.

O! lure of the Lost Lagoon,—
I dream tonight that my paddle blurs
The purple shade where the seaweed stirs,
I hear the call of the singing firs
In the hush of the golden moon.

PERSONAL JOURNAL

1. With a partner, look at the pattern of each stanza of the poem. A stanza is a "poetry paragraph." Can you find the pattern of the rhyme? Talk about the special outdoor places you each like to go to. Working together, or on your own, try writing poems about your special places. You can write a poem using this stanza pattern or you might prefer to use another form of poetry.

MEET STANISLAS RENOIR

Interviews are one important way to gather information from people. When do you think an interview would be best used? Are there times when interviews might not be one of the best ways of gathering information? Journals, diaries, and letters are sources of information too. Like interviews, these sources are good places to go when we are looking for information about how people feel.

Interaction, links, and influences are happening all around us. They happen in many different ways. One of these ways is when families move from one part of the world to another. You may have a friend who has moved to Canada from another part of the world.

Stan Renoir's family came from France. Now they live in Canada. Stan has many connections with France.

Stanislas Renoir is 12 years old. His family moved to Canada from France in 1978, just before he was born. Read the following interview with Stanislas to find out how his family is linked to France and to his home in Canada.

INTERVIEW

Q: Stanislas, why did your family decide to leave France?

"My parents moved to Canada with my grandparents, my great-grandmother, three uncles of mine, a dog, three cats, and a parrot. They told me they wanted to build something new."

Q: What kinds of things did you do when you first visited France to help yourself become "linked" to France?

"I visited my grandmother, my cousins, and friends. I went to the village, Puget-Theniers. This is where my mom grew up. I took sailing lessons in Nice, a town on the shores of the Mediterranean Sea."

Q: How has your Canadian lifestyle been influenced by the French way of life?

"I eat French food. My family speaks French at home. I play Petanque, *a game similar to lawn bowling, with my uncles, my father, and their friends."*

Q: What would you say have been the most positive ways that your family has been influenced by your move to Canada?

"I like the snow! I have traveled a lot and I speak different languages. I have made lots of new friends in both countries. My family is happy to be in Canada. There is a strong link between France and Canada. French Canadians have been in Canada for hundreds of years. My great-great-grandfather was Pierre Auguste Renoir. He is known for the paintings he did. He was part of a group of painters who all painted in the same way. This way was called Impressionism. Other painters that came after my great-great-grandfather influenced Canadian painters. You will read more about them in a later chapter."

Since he came to Canada, Stan has learned to ski. When he goes back to France for a visit, he may ski in the Alps.

Q: How do you stay in touch with events in France?

"One of my favourite sports is cycling. I always watch the Tour de France on tv. It is a very famous cycling competition in France. I'd like to tell you more about the Tour de France."

INTERVIEWER'S TOOLBOX

Interviews are one important way to gather information from people. When do you think an interview should be used? Are there times when interviews might not be one of the best ways of gathering information?

An interview allows you to collect first-hand information. Use this toolbox to help you plan and conduct your own interview. Interview one of your classmates. Keep the interview in your notebook.

Materials You Will Need

- pencil/pen
- paper or a tape-recorder to keep a record of the answers

Planning

- decide what you want to learn
- prepare your questions
- decide how you will record answers
- contact the person to be interviewed
- tell the person the purpose of the interview
- arrange a time for the interview

At the Interview

- introduce yourself
- share the questions you plan to ask
- ask the questions and record the answers
- thank the person for his or her help

Journals, diaries, and letters are sources of information too. Like interviews, these sources are good places to go when we are looking for information about how people feel.

THE TOUR DE FRANCE

The Tour de France bicycle race is the largest single sporting event in the world. Hundreds of people come from all over the world to take part. About 14 million people stand on the roadsides to see the racers speed by. Each year the route is changed, although there are some cities and mountain passes that are always visited.

The racers ride 3500 km in three weeks. The race is always held in July because France traditionally has a holiday shutdown in August. The only times the Tour de France has been cancelled were during the First and Second World Wars.

The Tour de France is for male cyclists and the Tour Feminin is for female cyclists. Both races go at the same time. American Marianne Martin bicycled into the record books by winning the first Tour Feminin in 1984.

Many people enjoy watching the Tour de France on tv. You might like to watch the race on tv too!

Bicycle racing is a popular sport all over the world. However, no race is as famous as the Tour de France!

On the following pages you will meet two more young people. Their families have ties to Britain and the United States. Great Britain was home to many thousands of people who decided to try their luck in the New World. Canada was part of that new world and the British came to settle here. Their ways of living were carried over to Canada. Ralph Perkins will describe how many of the traditions in Canada today come from Great Britain. Canada and the United States are neighbours and share many common interests. Wanda Lewis talks about some of these common interests. First, let's meet Ralph Perkins, from Scotland.

MEET RALPH PERKINS

"Where I grew up, in Perthshire, Scotland, everyone wore a uniform to school. Now that I'm living in Canada, I like to wear blue jeans to school. It is much colder here too, so I'm grateful to be able to pull on my **shetland wool** *sweater in the winter. In Scotland, the summers didn't seem as warm and dry as they are here. It's fun to visit the lakes here in Canada during the summer. My friend, Pete, has a summer cottage at Pigeon Lake. We go swimming and fishing there.*

"My grandmother came to Canada during World War II. She was one of thousands of kids

Many Canadians enjoy fishing. As Ralph says, "It's fun to visit the lakes in Canada."

who were sent here to be safe from the bomb threats. My grandmother and her brother were living in London, England at the time. London was bombed by the Germans during the war. Their parents wanted them out of the country at such a dangerous time. Many kids like my grandmother came to Canada. From that first visit, my family had a tie to Canada. Grandmother used to talk about her years in Halifax, Nova Scotia. She told us that "Nova Scotia" means "New Scotland." No wonder she felt so at home—with the ocean, the fishing, and the city life. After the war, my grandmother went back to Scotland. My mom heard her stories and always wanted to come to Canada. When a job at the university library opened up, she applied and we moved here to Alberta. It's fun to have my grandmother's tie to Canada, and to be making my own friendships in Canada. I still write to my friends in Perth.

"I also spend a lot of time reading adventure stories. Maybe I get my love for reading from Mom. She likes books so much that she became a librarian. We have many books in our home. You might like to know more about Scottish writers. I'd also like to tell you about a great Scottish sport, golf!"

The game of golf began in Scotland. Today thousands of Canadians enjoy the game!

SCOTTISH WRITERS

Have you ever read *Treasure Island* or *Kidnapped*? They were written by a Scotsman named Robert Louis Stevenson. Sir Walter Scott wrote *Ivanhoe*. Another story you may have read, or seen as a movie, is *Peter Pan*, written by Sir James Barrie.

GOLF

The people of Scotland have influenced us in sport as well. Scotland is a rugged country with many lakes and beautiful mountains. People there like to spend time outdoors. Perhaps that is why the Scottish invented the game of golf. At one time, golf was banned in Scotland because it was too popular! People preferred to play golf and not practise archery. In 1457, people had to practise archery so that they could defend the country! The oldest golf club in the world is at St. Andrews, Scotland. Today more people play golf than any other outdoor sport!

The stories, sports, and ideas have come together in Canada. As you read on, you will probably recognize the influence Wanda's favourite "playground" has had on the lives of Canadians.

MEET WANDA LEWIS

"School in Alberta is much the same as it was in Montana. One thing is different though: the way Canadians spell words like 'colour.' In the United States, people spell it 'color'!"

"Hi! My name is Wanda Lewis. I go to school in Calgary, Alberta. I am in grade 5. I have been in Canada since last June when we moved here from Billings, Montana. My dad is a football player. He is a linebacker with the CFL. That's the Canadian Football League. One of the things my whole family found different was the way football is played in Canada. In the NFL, or the National Football League, the rules are different. Anyway, it is a game that my dad loves and it is his job. That's why we're here.

"At some of the sports events we go to, there is a special show. Last year, we drove to Spruce Meadows to watch show jumping. At one of the intermissions, the Royal Canadian Mounted Police gave a musical ride. It was fun to watch!

"Montana is a lot like Alberta. I'm used to cold, snowy winters and to hot, dry summers. People here in Alberta speak with a different accent than I'm used to, but it's not that different. Have you ever visited the United States? Depending on where you go, people speak with different accents. I'm sure glad that I can still watch my favourite tv programs. I wonder why there are so many American shows on tv in Canada.

"Have you ever spent a family fun day at West Edmonton Mall, Calaway Park in Calgary, or Bedrock City in Kelowna? Theme parks and fantasy are a fairly new idea about how to spend leisure time. The idea began in the United States with a man named Walt Disney. When Mr. Disney's daughters were little, he used to take them to the playground or an amusement park near their home. The children seemed to have fun but it wasn't always a lot of fun for Mr. Disney. He decided that there should be parks that would be enormous fun for both parents and children."

The RCMP is Canada's own police force. Members of the force are also known as Mounties.

THE MAGICAL KINGDOM

In 1952, Walt Disney began to plan what his special park would have to be like. His hobby was model railways. In his own yard he had a track that was more than half a kilometre long! He really wanted his special park to have a railway that could move people around. This is where his idea started. Soon he had decided there would have to be a station at the beginning of the park. This would help people feel like they were entering a different world. Real towns have a main street near a railway station, so Main Street USA was added to the plan. When Disney added Sleeping Beauty's Castle, the Magical Kingdom was starting to take shape.

Walt Disney's idea for an amusement park was very successful. Do you recognize this castle from the Disney television show?

Walt Disney thought that people would stay interested and would have more fun if each street in the park took you to another theme. Themes would make it seem like you had stepped into another part of your imagination. Soon his park included Adventureland, Frontierland, Fantasyland, and Tomorrowland. Many imaginative people helped him build the ideas. In July of 1955, Disneyland in California was opened.

Every year, millions of people go to Disneyland. The idea of a family fun park for leisure was a good one. Even though people loved Disneyland just the way it was, Walt Disney never stopped thinking about ways to improve his idea. Over the years, new themes were added to Disneyland. Walt Disney had still more ideas so he began to plan a second park. He decided it should be built in another part of the United States. This way more people would be able to be a part of the fun. Today, Disney World is open in Florida.

Walt Disney was also a movie producer. He created the character of Mickey Mouse. Disney movies have included cartoons, adventure movies, and nature stories.

REPORT WRITING

1. Have you seen Disney Pictures' *White Fang*, or any other Disney film about Canada? Write a one page movie script or a description of a movie you would like to see about Canada.

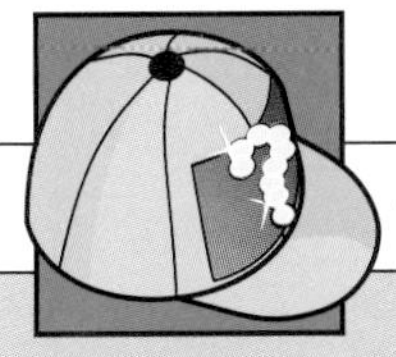

THINKING CAP

1. Do you think that Walt Disney's idea has influenced you, or a friend, or the community you live in?
2. What else can you say about how Walt Disney's idea has influenced leisure time?

CHAPTER WRAP-UP

You have seen that links can be made when people move from other countries to Canada. When people move from country to country, they bring some of the ways of their old country with them. One of the important things they often bring is a love for their old country. Once here, they change some of their ways to be more like Canadians. They often stay tied to family and friends. Telephone, mail, and travel help people stay connected even when they live far apart.

In this chapter, through the eyes of other children, you read about Canada. Marilyn Campbell is a Native Canadian. Unlike the other three children, she can trace her ancestors to this country. Her lifestyle bridges traditional Native customs with modern customs. She is equally at home in a canoe as in a car.

Stan Renoir was born shortly after his family moved to Canada from France. When his family came to Canada, they brought their language and customs with them. Stan's visits to France continue to tie him to his French heritage.

Ralph Perkins has adopted Canada as his new home. He is originally from Scotland. Ralph is reminded of his homeland whenever he sees someone playing golf, and when he reads novels by Scottish writers.

Wanda Lewis, the American girl, noticed certain differences between Canadians and Americans. Do you remember what they were? What were the similarities that she remarked on?

In the next chapter, you will read about traveling to the United States, Great Britain, and France.

ACTIVITIES

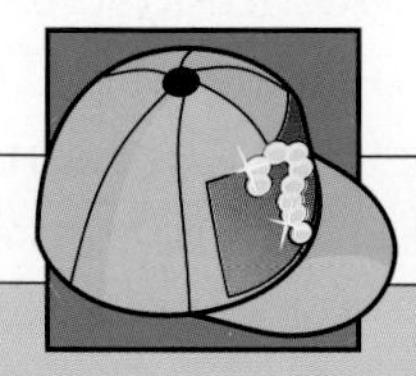

THINKING CAP

Asking good questions can save a lot of work. Some questions will let a person answer "Yes" or "No" even when you want more information. Good questions are the key to a successful interview. Let's look at the question words. You are probably familiar with using these six.

Who? What? Where? When? Why? How?

Test some of these words out. Try some combinations of your own. Make up your own interview questions to gather information about links people have with other countries and how they maintain the links.

PERSONAL JOURNAL

1. Write a poem or lyrics for a song about the idea, "It's a small world after all."
2. Write about a special way your family celebrates its cultural past.

INTERVIEW & SURVEY

As a class or in groups, conduct interviews to find out how many of your schoolmates have links to other countries in the world. In your investigation, try to identify some of the main ways that these links are maintained. Try to design at least three good questions that will encourage people to talk about themselves. Write your questions in your journal before you begin interviewing, or prepare a written interview form.

There is an example of an interview on page 42. An **Interviewer's Toolbox** is located on page 43. The **Thinking Cap** on page 48 might be helpful when you design your questions.

After you have finished the interviews, write down what you found out. Then analyse the information you gathered.

1. Are there similarities between what Stan shared and what you found in your interviews?
2. Is there anything you would do differently another time?
3. What worked especially well?

REPORT WRITING & OUTLINING

Look through magazines and newspapers to find an example of a Canadian who is making a contribution to our world. Write about why you think this person is making an important contribution.

CHAPTER 4

TRANSPORTATION AND TRADE

PREVIEW PAGE

From fishing ships bound for the New World, to moon-bound rocket ships, humans have traveled and explored. People create ways to transport themselves from one location to another. In this chapter, we will look at transportation and trade with other countries. Transportation and trade continue to affect how we influence and interact with each other. By traveling, we can get to know each other. We can form bonds or ties with people from other cultures. Transportation and trade strengthen Canada's ties to the United States, France, and Britain. In this chapter we will transport you on a tour of these three countries.

BENEFITS OF TRANSPORTATION

In chapter 2 you learned that some links in history were formed because of exploration and trade. In many ways, bonds are formed between countries today for the same reasons as in the past. In modern times, transportation plays the same role in linking the people of the world through travel. Of course, humans have explored the surface of the Earth. Today curiosity ties countries together as they explore outer space. Working together on new technologies for space links countries.

Transportation is also closely tied to trade. Trade has become easier because of the new technologies in transportation. Large ships, railway systems, cargo planes, and highway systems make it easier for goods to move between places. Now that we know how to use refrigeration, we can move many **perishable** foods from place to place. Imagine life without pineapple from the state of Hawaii or juicy oranges from California or Florida!

Today, people in countries like Canada are used to enjoying foods and trade goods from almost every country in the world. Without transportation, this would not be possible. It is the same for people in other countries too. Did you know that trade was the main reason that the Chunnel was built? People wanted to make trade easier between the islands of Britain and the rest of the countries in Europe.

In modern times, people travel for many reasons. They travel to do business and to participate in sports. They also travel to meet and discuss issues. Sometimes people travel because they are moving their home from one part of the world to another. Other times they travel for the pleasure of seeing another part of our world. How do you use transportation in your life? How has transportation helped you link with other people and places?

Highways link people and places together. Trade between countries is made easier by having more transportation routes.

In the years of exploration and settlement, the French and the British traveled by boat, on foot, and on horseback. Those first ships took weeks to complete the journey. Times have changed! Large luxury ships travel across the oceans. Most of the large passenger ships have swimming pools, movie theatres, and tennis courts. Some even have ice cream stands on board! Today you can travel by airplane from almost anywhere in Canada to England in less than 10 hours. Another hour and you can fly over the Eiffel Tower in Paris, France. Just a few hours on a large jet will take you to Disneyland or to a beach in Hawaii.

THE CHUNNEL

The name Chunnel is a mixture of the words channel, for English Channel, and tunnel, the chunnel built under the English Channel. The Chunnel is a tunnel that connects England and France underneath the ocean floor. Trucks and cars can drive onto moveable platforms at stations located on either side of the ocean. Passengers can get out and have a snack in the cafeteria while they are ferried along the underground tracks. Train tracks also run through the Chunnel. Do you think that it is possible that tunnels might one day be built to connect the continents of North America and Europe?

When the Chunnel is completed, people will be able to drive from France to England. They will be able to drive right into London.

DESIGN YOUR OWN ICON

1. Use the following dialogue to make an illustration. Your drawing will show that not everyone thinks the tunnel link from Britain and France is a great idea. Some people, especially in Britain, like living on islands. They feel the short distance by water or plane is not troublesome for visiting and trading. The British feel more British when they are separated from **the continent**.

   The Lion: *We take pride in our heritage and in the fact that we live on a unique island.*

   The Rooster: *But think how much easier and less costly it will be for us to visit each other by tunnel!*

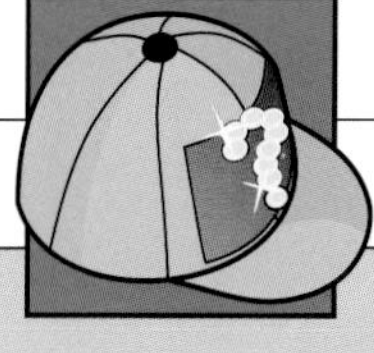

THINKING CAP

1. What do you think of the Chunnel?
2. Do you think established borders are important for good relationships between countries? Or do you think that borders are barriers that prevent people from really getting to know each other?

FROM COVERED WAGONS TO THE CONCORDE

Many people take modern transportation for granted. When you read the following account, you will get another point of view. Catherine Parr Traill, a Canadian pioneer, moved from a wealthy British family to live in Upper Canada with her husband. She was a writer and a **botanist** who kept a detailed journal of her observations and findings in this new land of wonders. She wrote in *Backwoods of Canada*:

> *Our progress was but slow on account of the roughness of the road, which is* **beset** *with* **innumerable obstacles** *in the shape of loose blocks of limestone, with which the lands on the banks of the river and lakes abound; to say nothing of fallen trees, big roots, mud-holes, and* **corduroy bridges** *over which you go jolt, jolt, jolt, till every bone in your body feels as if it were being dislocated. An experienced bush-traveller avoids many hard thumps by rising up or clinging to the sides of his rough vehicle.*
>
> *As the day was particularly fine, I often* **quitted the wagon** *and walked on with my husband for a mile* [1.6 km] *or so.*

Wouldn't Catherine Parr Traill be surprised if she could see how humans travel now? Super highways replace the difficult trails she traveled on.

While Catherine Parr Traill was writing her diary, the modern bicycle was being invented. A bicycle-type machine was invented in France and improved in Scotland.

The Concorde is the fastest passenger airplane on Earth. Using the Concorde can get you from Canada to France or Britain in record time.

By the late 1800s, European roads were built so that cyclists could travel back and forth.

One of the greatest inventions was the car. Henry Ford, an American, built his first car at the end of the 1800s. Think of how the car has influenced life in Canada.

Fantastic attempts to make travel easier and faster continue today. The Concorde **supersonic** airliner is a perfect example of how humans have tried to make international transportation faster.

The idea of the Concorde was dreamed up in Britain on November 5, 1956 by the Supersonic Transport Aircraft Committee. It was a very expensive idea. Britain asked the United States, France, and Germany if they would help to pay for the Concorde jet. France agreed to help, even though Britain and France have different languages, traditions, and **systems of measurement**. In Britain, measuring weights is done in ounces and pounds. In France, it's done in grams and kilograms. Each country also had its own factory using its own system of measurement. Somehow Britain and France overcame these differences. The Concorde was finally built and tested. It flew from Washington to Paris in a record-breaking time of 3 hours and 33 minutes. It usually takes 8 to 10 hours to fly from North America to Europe! This airplane can fly at twice the speed of sound. The average speed of a Concorde is 1752 kilometres per hour.

TRADE LINKS

You have read about the fur trade and the links it created. Trade is an important way for Canada to stay linked with Great Britain, France, and the United States. Each country trades things it makes. Cars, clothing, and electronic equipment are traded. Countries also trade food like grains, fruits and vegetables, and meat and fish.

Natural resources are also traded between countries. Oil and natural gas, wood products, and water are bought and sold. Trade happens when a country needs something another country produces. Trade happens when a country has enough extra of something that another country might be interested in buying.

Countries also try to make money through trade. In a way, a country is something like a family. It costs money for your family to live well. In a family, someone usually works to earn money to trade for the things the family needs. Working is a way people trade the knowledge or special skills that they have for money. Countries need money too. Countries earn money through trade. Mostly countries trade **goods** and **raw materials** to earn money. The more money a country earns through trade, the better the *standard of living* will probably be for the people who live in the country. The standard of living is how well most of the people in a country are able to live.

Goods and raw materials that a country buys are called *imports*. Goods and raw materials that a country sells are called *exports*. Trade is made up of imports and exports. Canada trades many goods and raw materials with Great Britain, France, and the United States. Goods are things that have been made, and raw materials are what is used to make something else. A nail is called a good because it is a finished thing. The metal that is used to make the nail is called the raw material.

GRAPH-MAKER'S TOOLBOX

There are four main kinds of graphs.

1. Line graphs are used to show how things change.

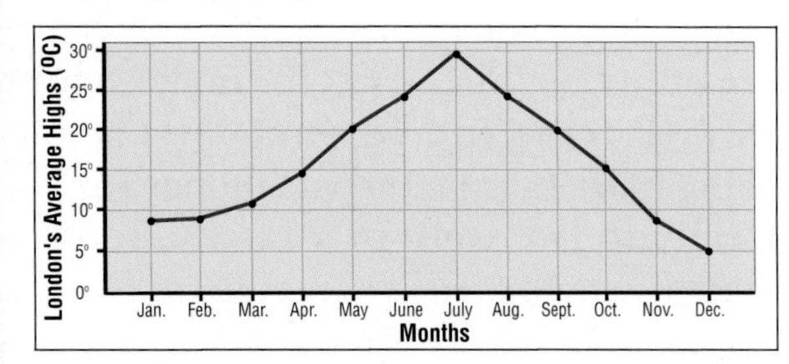

This graph shows the change in temperature.

2. Circle graphs are used to show how a whole thing has been divided.

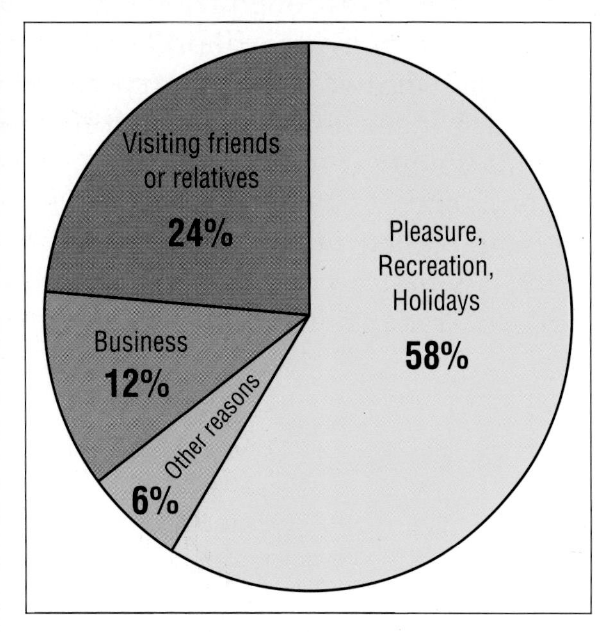

This graph shows the reasons why Canadians travel to the United States.

3. Bar graphs are used to compare things.

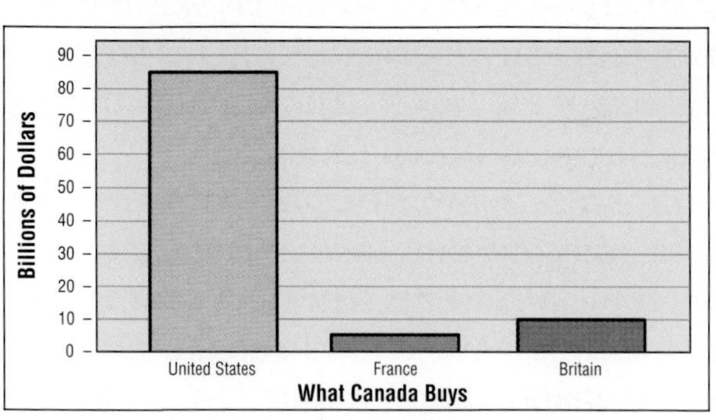

This graph compares the differences in imports sold to Canadians by the United States, Great Britain, and France.

4. Pictographs are bar graphs that use pictures.

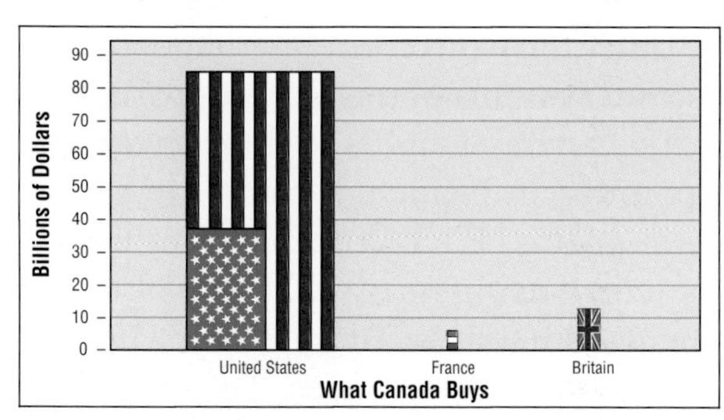

This graph shows the same thing as the bar graph only it has used pictures.

Planning

- what do I want to show?
- what kind of graph will work best?

Materials

- graph paper or unlined paper
- ruler or compass

Making Your Graph

- label the two sides or the sections of your graph
- include a title

USING CHARTS

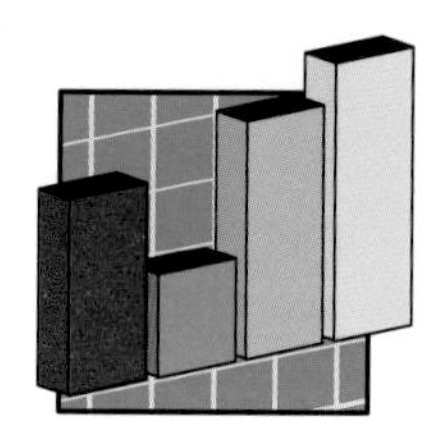

Study the charts below. The one chart shows some of the goods and raw materials that Canada imports from Great Britain, France, and the United States. The other chart shows some of the goods and raw materials that Canada exports to Great Britain, France, and the United States. Canada produces a **surplus** of some goods. Can you tell which goods these are? What does this tell you about the other countries? Using the information on the charts, did Canada spend more money or make more money by trading with these three countries?

WHAT CANADA SELLS

Country	Items	Total Cost
The United States	lumber, wood pulp, oil, natural gas, hydro-electric energy, aluminum, cars, car engines, aircraft parts	$101 billion
France	lumber, wood pulp, salmon, lobster, iron ore, chemicals, airplane engines, office machinery, telecommunications equipment	$1.2 billion
Great Britain	lumber, softwood, wood pulp, newsprint, salmon, nickel, iron, copper, chemicals, telecommunications equipment	$3.6 billion

WHAT CANADA BUYS

Country	Items	Total Cost
The United States	cars, car engines, aircraft parts, coal, bulldozers, cranes, computers, fresh fruit and vegetables, clothing	$86.5 billion
France	aircraft, automobiles, steel bars, cheese, perfume, wine	$2.9 billion
Great Britain	crude oil, transportation equipment, cutlery, china, leather	$4.6 billion

FREE TRADE

Countries want the people in their country to buy goods that are made there. Cars are an example of this idea. The government of Canada would like Canadians to buy cars that are made in Canada. Buying things that are made in your own country helps give jobs to the people of your country. At the same time, most governments believe that people should have choices. For a long time, countries had special taxes that were added to the price of goods and raw materials that were brought in from other countries. This meant that you could choose to buy things that came from other countries but you would have to pay extra for them.

From the charts, you can see that Canada does a lot of trading with the United States. For many years, taxes were added onto the cost of goods and raw materials traded between Canada and the United States. In 1988, the prime minister of Canada and the president of the United States changed the way trade would take place between their two countries. They did this when they signed the Free Trade Agreement. The Free

Since Henry Ford created the first mass-produced automobiles, cars have become part of our everyday lives. Cars make up a large part of the trade that links countries.

Trade Agreement is a special contract between Canada and the United States. It allows many goods and raw materials to be traded between the two countries without the extra taxes. Great Britain, France, and many of the other countries of Europe have an agreement similar to free trade. These European countries have joined together to form a group called the European Economic Community (EEC).

DESIGN YOUR OWN ICON

1. Draw a cartoon of the Beaver and the Eagle discussing free trade.

   Beaver: *The United States has 10 times the population of Canada. How are Canadians supposed to compete with lower American prices?*

   Eagle: *Free trade between the United States and Canada will allow goods to move more freely across the border.*

EDITORIAL

1. Compare free trade between the United States and Canada to the Chunnel between Britain and France.
2. Do you think free trade between Canada and the United States is helpful or harmful to friendly relations?
3. Do you think Canada is lucky to have such a big neighbour? Why or why not?

TRAVEL LINKS

Modern-day transportation allows people to travel when they want and wherever they want. People travel for many different reasons. Tourism has become so popular that it has created many new businesses and jobs for people. Does this surprise you? Travel has become so much a part of modern life that we now have travel **agencies**, tour companies, and luggage manufacturers. Can you think of other changes that are due to tourism?

USING GRAPHS

Canadians travel a lot! Most of our travel is to the United States. Can you think of a reason for this? By the end of the 1980s, Canadians were crossing the borders to the United States more than 45 million times a year. Since Canada has a population of less than 30 million people, this means that more than half the people made more than one trip. Check your class. How many trips were made by your classmates and their families?

This graph shows reasons why Canadians traveled to the United States. Study the graph to see what is the most common reason for travel. What do you think might be "other reasons" for travel?

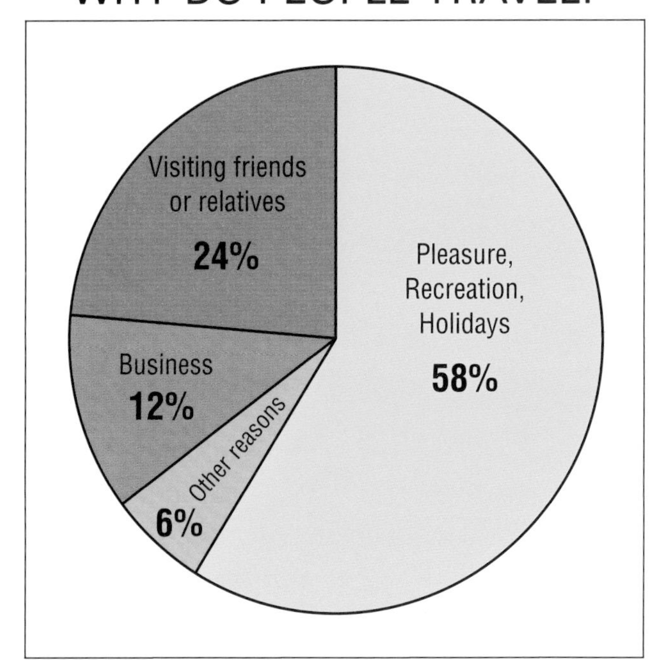

Travelers come to Canada from all over the world. Most of the travelers coming to Canada are from the United States. Millions of Americans cross the borders into Canada every year. As well, nearly 3 million overseas travelers come to Canada every year.

LET'S TAKE A TRIP

Travel links us to other places in many ways. Business travelers need to know about the language used by the people with whom they will be doing business. It is important to know about the customs of the people in order to use good manners. Climate will influence what clothing should be packed.

Tourists need to know the same things as business travelers. They also need to plan the kind of trip they would like to have. Some people travel to learn about the history of a place. Others want to learn about the way other people in our world are living. There are tourists who like to participate in sports while they travel. By planning ahead, people are preparing to interact with new people and new places. The planning will also influence many of the decisions the traveler will make.

Knowing what to pack for your trip is important.

PERSONAL JOURNAL

1. The pages that follow outline three different tours, to our neighbours Great Britain, France, and the United States. Plan a similar tour for Canada. Keep the tour in your personal journal.

TIPS FOR THE TRAVELER—GREAT BRITAIN

Language: English
*petrol = gasoline
*wireless = radio
*lorries = trucks
*lifts = elevators

Currency: pound

Sporting Events:
cricket
soccer
rugby
football

Climate: (London)

Month	Average Temperature (Celsius)	Days of Rain/Snow
January	5	17
February	5	13
March	7	11
April	9	14
May	15	13
June	17	11
July	19	13
August	19	13
September	15	13
October	11	14
November	6	16
December	4	16

Typical Breakfast: tea, kippers (smoked herring)

Famous For: theatre, pop concerts, museums

MARISSA IN ENGLAND

"Hi. My name is Marissa. My mom and I just came back from a trip to England and to France. It's neat over there. Our first stop was in London. It's one of the world's largest cities. It's so big it has two international airports—Gatwick and Heathrow. We landed at Gatwick Airport. Charles, the English man who sat with Mom and me, asked us whether we were staying in London or moving on to another place. We said we were going to a town north of London called High Wycombe. It's about three hours away from Gatwick by train and taxi cabs. Charles was stunned we were going there. England has hundreds of villages and towns we could have been visiting, but it turned out that High Wycombe was exactly where Charles was going too. It was really weird. Charles told us to come along with him. Mom said he was like an angel without wings because he guided us through train connections and hailed cabs for us.

"I was so tired from jet lag. It's called jet lag because when you travel to different countries you also travel through different time zones. England is seven hours ahead of Edmonton, Alberta.

"The people we were staying with in High Wycombe were really fun. Juliet is a fashion designer; one of her clients is Cyndi Lauper. Steven is an antique dealer. Their house is all brick and has huge roses growing around it, and Old English Ivy growing over their door. They have neat words that we don't use in Canada. Like the bathroom is called the loo, and sweaters are called jumpers.

"We went into London with them to have tea with the Queen . . . joke . . . we just saw where she lived. It's called Buckingham Palace. We saw Big Ben, the Tower of London, Hyde Park, Portobello Road—which is a huge street market—and lots of places that are historical. They also have modern buildings in London.

"The street market at Portobello Road was fun! I bought a copper bracelet there."

"It's different than in Canada, because they have some buildings that are centuries old, and others that were just built. We went on underground trains. Londoners call it taking the tube.

"You wouldn't believe most of the roads. They're so narrow. Mom says it's because land is so precious there, they don't want to give too much of it away to roads. You don't see very many big cars there. The whole country of Britain could fit into the province of Alberta. They also drive on the left side of the road. And the steering wheel is on the right-hand side of the car. It feels a little scary at first till you get used to it.

"Our next stop was to see friends in the south part of England. Laura and Anne live in a little village called Sixpenny Lane. It's between a resort town called Bournemouth and the famous town of Salisbury. Salisbury is supposed to have the tallest church spire in England. The thing I noticed about driving in the English countryside is that every few kilometres or, as the British say, miles, there is a little town or village. Beside the narrow roads are rock fences, beautiful hedges, and canopies of overhanging trees.

"After our visit we doubled back toward London but went on to Dover because we wanted to take a boat to France. Dover is famous for its white cliffs that face the English Channel. The English Channel between Dover and Calais, France is about 15 kilometres wide. The water was choppy so it took us about an hour to get across by hovercraft."

TIPS FOR THE TRAVELER—FRANCE

Language: French
*bonjour = hello
*au revoir = goodbye
*s'il vous plaît = please
*merci = thank you

Currency: franc

Sporting Events:
Tour de France (July)
soccer
Grand Prix

Climate: (Paris)

Month	Average Temperature (Celsius)	Days of Rain/Snow
January	6	15
February	4	13
March	7	15
April	1	14
May	14	13
June	17	11
July	19	12
August	19	12
September	16	11
October	11	14
November	6	15
December	4	17

Typical Breakfast: café au lait, croissants or brioches (soft rolls), butter, jam

Famous For: haute cuisine (fine gourmet cooking)

MARISSA IN FRANCE

"As soon as Mom and I landed in France we knew we were in a different country. It's amazing that, while Britain and France aren't far from each other, they're so different. Mom says, France has a certain air to it. Of course the first thing we noticed was everyone speaks French. We speak French a little bit. It's not easy being in a country where you don't know the language very well. I decided when I got back to Canada I would be more understanding with people who are learning English.

"Our big stop in France was Paris. Like Britain, it has a mixture of really old buildings and new buildings. They drive fast over there! I thought to myself, at least they drive on the same side of the road as Canadians. We stayed at a bed and breakfast place on the Left Bank. Paris is split into two banks—the right and the left. The Left Bank is supposed to be less fancy, but more trendy. The Sorbonne University is there, and really cool boutiques, bookstores, and cafés with street umbrella tables, and artists selling their work on the sidewalks. It was a busy section of the city. All night long I could hear car horns honking. The city doesn't sleep. London has the River Thames running through it. Paris has the Seine. Commercial and pleasure boats go up and down both rivers. I thought how different it was from rivers in Alberta. I hardly ever see anything on our river in Edmonton.

"Mom and I went to see some really awesome buildings like the Eiffel Tower, Arc de Triomphe, Notre Dame Cathedral, and the Louvre. The Louvre is a massive art gallery and museum. We could have stayed days just going through that one building. We walked a lot. It's a great city to roam around in. I noticed in the parks that people were really careful not to walk on the grass. They kept mainly on the sidewalks. There was a big fountain in one park we walked to, and a bunch of kids were floating miniature sailboats.

"In Paris, artists work and sell their paintings right on the street!"

They have beautiful gardens there. Mom kept taking pictures of their flowers and big trees.

"Another thing that I noticed in Paris was that there weren't any single or separate houses. All the houses I saw around central Paris were **attached**. They have small backyards that are like **courtyards**. I suppose that some of the Paris **suburbs** have single houses, but we didn't see any until we left Paris. One other thing—the food is great.

"Mom wanted me to see some of France's countryside, so we took a tour down to the Loire Valley. This is France's winegrowing region. It's beautiful. There were castles, and grand estates. The towns all had big churches, and the people seem keen on knowing about their history. France also has regional accents, just like in Britain. Mom said she noticed her French was more like the French used in Paris than the French we heard as we traveled into France's southern region.

"The second city we went to in France was Nice. The coast view along the Mediterranean Sea is . . . hmm, to quote my mom . . . absolutely staggering. Lush greens and blues, and a feeling that people are enjoying luxury and life to the fullest.

"Would I like to visit France and Britain again? I certainly would, but I have to say one last thing about traveling—it also makes you appreciate home."

PERSONAL JOURNAL

1. Why do you think Marissa says traveling makes you appreciate home? Can you think of a time this was true for you? Record your answers in your personal journal.

TIPS FOR THE TRAVELER—THE UNITED

Language: English
*zee = zed
*scam = fraud
*yup = yes
*bathrobe = dressing gown

Currency: US dollar

Sporting Events:
baseball
football
hockey

Climate: (New Orleans)

Month	Average Temperature (Celsius)	Days of Rain/Snow
January	11	5
February	12	5
March	16	4
April	20	4
May	24	5
June	27	4
July	28	6
August	27	6
September	25	5
October	20	2
November	15	4
December	12	5

Typical Breakfast: café au lait and hot beignets (hot milk with coffee and hot donuts covered in icing sugar)

Famous For: Mardi Gras, jazz music, Mississippi River

LOUISIANA... *COME TOUR OUR TOWNS!*

Pack your bags for one of America's finest tours back in time. You're on your way to **plantation** country!

Why not start your exploration of Louisiana in New Orleans? That's right, the Mardi Gras Festival city is right here. Two weeks of make-believe, parades, fantastic costumes, and fun, fun, fun! And while you're at it, get your taste buds ready. Our Cajun cooking is hot and spicy. **Gumbo** is a specialty.

Louisiana has that special French flavour; in its love of life and its lifestyle. Back in the eighteenth century many of the French from Nova Scotia left Canada. They journeyed south and it was here they stopped. They called the area "Acadiana." Their **descendants** still live here. Many of the people speak Cajun French—a French that hasn't changed in nearly 200 years.

From New Orleans, take a cruise boat up the great Mississippi River. Stop to wonder at the great plantation homes. Or, if you like the mysteries of nature, visit one of the swamps to see rare birds, alligators, and the great cypress trees.

And while you're here . . . check it out:

- creole cooking and jazz music
- St. Peter's Cathedral
- the French Quarter
- the Aquarium of the Americas
- Bastille Day
- Hodges Gardens
- Toledo Bend Lake for bass fishing
- much, much more!

STATES - Louisiana

New Orleans is famous for its Mardi Gras Festival. It's fun!

PERSONAL JOURNAL

1. Would you like to visit the state of Louisiana? Why or why not?
2. Locate Louisiana on a map of the United States. From the map, what can you tell about the climate?
3. Make a list of what you would have to pack for this trip.

CHAPTER WRAP-UP

In this chapter we reviewed the important role transportation plays in tying people and countries together. People need transportation for travel, as well as for importing and exporting goods and services.

Now, more than ever, people are traveling to almost every part of the world. When people connect or interact, they influence each other. Sometimes how we influence each other can be positive; other times it can be negative, especially if we do not respect other people's points of view or customs. Our tour to England, France, and to the United States showed that differences between people can be interesting. Don't you think it would be a boring place if we all looked alike and thought the same things?

In this chapter we also studied Canada's trade relationship with the United States, Britain, and France. Although we trade with most countries in the world, the United States is our major trading partner. Approximately 70 per cent of our trade is with the United States. Because Canada depends on the United States so much, the Americans have tremendous influence over our economy and how we think.

Like all countries in the world, Canada needs trading partners. If Canada didn't have trading partners, it would have a shortage of certain items, such as fruit in the winter. Canada also trades its goods to other countries. Importing and exporting is how governments make money.

We may trade **material goods**, but we can also trade information and ideas with other people. The exchange or trading of information, feelings, and ideas is examined in the next chapter when we study communication and culture.

ACTIVITIES

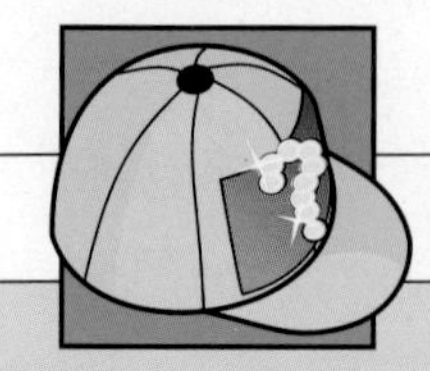

THINKING CAP

What does Canada trade with other countries? What are the reasons that countries trade goods and services? Why do people in your community travel?

Try participating in problem solving. Problem solving is a strategy used when we want to find an answer to a question or problem. When people take the time to search out the facts, they usually become informed about something they did not know a great deal about. Sometimes people confirm the information they already knew.

Problem solving involves several steps. They are

- understand what the question or problem is asking
- develop questions for research (example: What goods do Canadians need?)
- make a research plan
- gather and organize your information
- examine and interpret the information
- come to a conclusion or solution

PERSONAL JOURNAL

In your journal, try one of these activities or an activity that your teacher suggests for you.

Write about what you think is the most important form of transportation for linking people in modern times. Do you think this form of transportation has made life better or worse for the people that have been linked? Why? Describe a travel tour to a part of Canada. Be sure to describe what you think a tourist might be interested in seeing and doing.

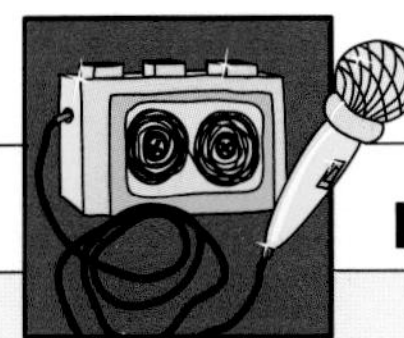

INTERVIEW & SURVEY

Take the role of a newspaper reporter. Use an interview to help you find out how someone you know feels about the last trip he or she took. Try to design at least three good questions that will encourage a person to talk about what he or she feels. Write your questions in your journal before you conduct the interview. Leave space to record what is said!

There is an example of an interview on page 42. An **Interviewer's Toolbox** is located on page 43. The **Thinking Cap** on page 48 might be helpful when you design your questions.

CHAPTER 5

MODERN CONNECTIONS: COMMUNICATION AND CULTURE

PREVIEW PAGE

Technology in modern times has added to the ways we can communicate. Television has become a part of most of our lives. We can watch programs that are made in one part of the world because of cable and satellite tv.

Communication makes it possible for the people of the world to learn about each other. One way that people living in a country can be described is through their culture. Culture includes the language of a group of people. It also includes the way people spend their free time, the style of clothing they wear, and their music. Culture includes many other things that have to do with the way that a group of people enjoy living together.

Communication makes it possible for people to share ideas and information. Communication can take place in a variety of ways. Conversations take place between people when they are together. Telephones, radios, and walkie-talkies allow people to use speech to communicate even when they are in different locations. Writing is another way to communicate with others. Letters, books, magazines, and newspapers are just a few of the many ways we can communicate in writing. Fax machines can send a piece of writing around the world in a matter of minutes!

Letter writing is one of the many ways we can communicate.

As we discovered in chapter 4, the more contact people have with each other, the more they influence each other. Cultural activities are forms of communication. Dance, art, writing, film, music, and theatre are some examples of cultural activities. Can you think of any others?

Ballet is one kind of cultural activity. Canada has several ballet troupes who perform in other parts of the world.

The cultural activities of a people tell us a story about what the people value. For example, a country might be famous for its wonderful restaurants and a special way of cooking. This might tell you that the people value taking time to enjoy good food with good friends.

The cultural activities a people value give them an identity. Think back to the last chapter. What did you learn about the identity of Britain, France, and the United States?

In Canada, we are able to enjoy many different cultural activities. Like our other world neighbours, these activities tell a story about what Canadians value. They are part of the Canadian identity.

When we meet people from other cultures, we naturally share ideas and communicate. Sometimes, the ideas will influence the beliefs we have. In this chapter, we will explore some of the many ways that culture has been shared or **adopted** by Canadians. As you read, think about the advantages and disadvantages you see.

In this chapter, we will explore music as one form of culture. We will also look at how sharing ideas and culture influences people.

FILM, TELEVISION, AND VIDEO

Do you spend part of your free time watching movies, television, or videos? Did you realize that much of what you watch is made in the United States? You have probably heard about the famous movie studios found in Hollywood, California. Many of our tv shows are also produced in Hollywood.

Canadians are working to become more involved in producing films and videos. Each year, Canada produces new tv programs. Telefilm Canada is a government company working to help Canadians. Sometimes Telefilm Canada gives money to help make a film or television show. This company also helps people from different countries take part in filmmaking.

One of the projects that Telefilm Canada helped with was *Babar: The Movie*. This movie was **co-produced** by filmmakers from Canada and France. Do you know the Babar stories written by Jean de Brunoff? If you do not know these stories, you will be able to find them in a library that has a youth section. The television series, "The Campbells," is co-produced by Canada and Great Britain. Another program you might recognize is "Anne of Green Gables." This television movie was co-produced by Canada and the United States.

This photograph shows a film crew working on a Canadian movie called High Country. *Can you guess what some of the people are doing?*

Television, films, and videos tell stories with pictures. Stories often show the way a group of people live. As we see stories from other countries, we become influenced. This happens as we learn more about other people and come to better understand them. It also happens as we hear new expressions or get new ideas about how to do something. For example, when Anne of Green Gables decides to try to dye her red hair raven black, she learns a lesson. Reading the book or watching the movie about how Anne's hair turns green could influence you! Would you buy hair dye from someone and try to change your hair colour?

COMMUNICATION

In the early days—before typewriters, computers, telephones, and fast planes— people mainly had to communicate in more simple ways and to fewer people. For example, North American Native people used **oral** communication. They shared their history through legends, songs, and traditional customs. The ways they went about their daily lives communicated their beliefs and culture.

When North American settlers wanted to contact people in Europe, they had to handwrite letters and send them by ship. Even with this technology, it would take weeks, sometimes months, before letters would reach their **destinations**.

The telegraph and the telephone were invented as people worked to find better and faster ways to communicate over distances. The telephone was invented by Alexander Graham Bell in 1876. Bell was a Canadian. How do you think his invention has influenced people around the world?

It was not until modern times that messages could be sent across the oceans. In 1956, the first telephone cables linked Canada and Great Britain. People still continued to look for ways to improve distance communication. Satellites were one new idea in technology that helped. In the next section, you will read more about this modern connection: the satellite!

Today, satellites improve our communications. We can thank this technology for allowing us to communicate faster and more easily than in the past.

TELECOMMUNICATIONS: A SATELLITE ADVENTURE

The first experiments with satellite communications began in the United States. Scientists discovered that communication beams could be sent into space and bounced back to Earth off satellites. By changing the tilt of the satellite, messages would bounce back at different angles. NASA, the American space organization, put the first communications satellite in space on December 18, 1958. NASA also helped Canada to put a communications satellite in space on September 29, 1962. In the next chapter you will have a chance to see many other ways that Canada has worked with other countries in space.

Satellites can help send sound messages around the world. They can also help send messages you can see. Try watching the television news at supper time. Did any of the people reading the news say, "We will now go to our reporter, live from Toronto"? The expression, "live from," is a clue that the picture you are seeing has just taken a trip through space before making its way to you. Being able to send words and pictures around the world has meant that Canadians can be linked with their world neighbours.

The rest of this chapter shows how some parts of cultures have moved between countries. As you read, try to decide which forms of communication have been most important in passing messages.

HOW SATELLITES WORK

Sender A sends out a signal to the satellite. The satellite sends the signal down to receiver B. In this way, messages can be sent around the world.

FADS INFLUENCE YOU!

Have you ever had a friend introduce you to a new kind of food or music or way of dressing? Have you ever thought, "That's neat! I want to be like that," or, "That is so great, I've just got to have one"? If you have, you have probably been influenced by an idea that began with someone else. Being influenced is a normal part of our life.

The skateboard was created in the 1960s. By the 1970s, it was a worldwide craze!

Canada has new people moving here every day from all over the world. We also have an excellent communications system that allows Canadians to be world watchers. This means we can see what is happening worldwide through television, newspapers, and magazines. As world watchers, we know the latest fashions, who the new musical groups are, and how the sports teams in other countries are doing.

Fads are a type of influence. Fads can be a big part of growing up. You have probably become a part of the fad connection. Fads can be a way of talking, a hairstyle, or a way that you spend your time after school. Most fads are harmless and are just fun. Other fads are dangerous. Some fads catch on and end up becoming a permanent part of our lifestyle. Others last for a few months and are forgotten.

Can you think of a time when you have heard a parent, a teacher, or a member of the clergy caution you about a fad? When we are faced with new ideas, we have a challenge. Not all influences are good for us. Individuals must make decisions about whether or not a fad is good. Countries must do the same thing. The rest of this chapter describes some of the fads young people in Canada have tried. As you look at them, take on the challenge. Examine the facts and form a personal opinion.

As you read the following Case Study, think about fads. Many fads are communicated through ads you see on tv or hear on the radio. At the end of this Case Study, you will be asked some questions. Be ready to put on your thinking cap!

CASE STUDY: *ADS*

Norman was completely won over by an advertisement he saw in a magazine about a cigarette brand. The guy in the ad looked so cool, so tough, and his girlfriend was so gorgeous. Norman figured maybe cigarette smoking would make him look more macho. He went out that day and got some cigarettes. It was not a pleasant experience. He thought he would either choke or throw up when he tried smoking. That was it for Norm. He decided that it would be better to accept himself the way he was. He didn't think half choking every time he took a drag on a cigarette would make him look cool at all.

PERSONAL JOURNAL

Throughout *Canadian Connections*, you have been challenged to form your own opinions. You have seen that forming opinions is a responsible way to show what we know and how we feel about what we know. Have you noticed that fads ask us to feel one particular way? A fad often becomes successful when it begins with an advertising campaign.

Advertising always has a message. Sometimes the ad is asking us to do something. Other times an ad will be asking us to buy something. It is easy to be caught up in the excitement of ads. When this happens, we sometimes let the ad make our decision for us. It can turn out to be a poor decision. Even with ads, we need to form our own opinions first. Ads can help us as long as we take time to find the message.

Finding the message is usually not that difficult. When Norman saw the ad about smoking, he could have asked these questions.

1. What is the ad asking me to do?
2. Is this something that will be good for me?
3. How?
4. Are there any tricks or problems?
5. Would people I respect have other ideas?

Try out the strategy. Answer the questions for Norman. Record your answers in your Personal Journal.

You might want to watch an ad on Saturday morning tv. Watch the ad carefully then ask yourself the questions. If possible, watch the ad a second time. This will help you confirm your findings. Be prepared to share your findings with your classmates.

LEISURE LIVING

We spend our time in many different ways. Take a minute to think about how you spend a normal day. What do you do with your time? Do you do different things with your time during holidays? Do you take vacations with your family? Is there a place you have always wanted to travel to for a holiday? As you read about leisure living, you will see how the way we spend our time may be changed by the ideas of other people.

How do you like to spend your leisure time?

Work and leisure are two important ways we spend our time. Our work time has many responsibilities. It needs a lot of energy in order for us to do our very best. Going to school can be thought of as one of the first important and responsible jobs that people have.

Canadians believe that leisure time is also an important part of a good life. Leisure time can help us relax and can be a fun part of life. Most people in Canada try to have a balance in their work and leisure time.

Leisure time can be spent playing or reading or enjoying friends. You can probably think of many other enjoyable ways to use leisure time. People in countries like Canada, Great Britain, France, and the United States have given a lot of thought to interesting ways we might spend our leisure time. France is known for wonderful summer bike trips through the countryside. Some of the best plays in the world can be found in London, England and in New York City, USA. The United States is also home to one of the most famous leisure ideas in the world. You read about Disneyland in chapter 3. How has Disney influenced you, a friend, or the people in the community you live in?

INTERVIEW & SURVEY

1. Interview a classmate who has been to Disneyland. Ask what he or she thought of Disneyland. What did he or she like most about the adventure? What, if anything, did he or she not like about Disneyland?

FAST FOOD

Eating can be a part of leisure time. It may be hard to believe, but fast food has been around for a long time! Thousands of years ago, the ancient Romans had one of the first types of fast food. They had food stands where they could buy a quick meal that came all in one dish. Did you ever think of the sandwich as being a fast food? It is! The sandwich began in Britain. There are people who study how the fast food fad has grown. They believe that the sandwich was an important invention. Why do you think the sandwich is classified as a fast food?

One of the most famous fast food fads is (can you guess?) McDonald's. McDonald's is important for more than its hamburgers. The McDonald's ideas about fast food have influenced people all over the world. Read the Case Study about McDonald's. Examine how McDonald's contributed to the fast food fad.

CASE STUDY: *McDONALD'S*

In the following Case Study about McDonald's, think about how much influence this concept has had on people. McDonald's restaurants are now located throughout the world. The McDonald's arch is a symbol that is recognized by people from many different cultures.

McDonald's began in the state of California. The owners were two brothers, Richard and Maurice McDonald. They began with a fast food stand that sold hamburgers, cheeseburgers, milk, pop, pie, and potato chips. Customers asked to have French fries and milkshakes added to the menu. The stand was different from other hamburger stands. The food was prepared on counters in the middle of the stand. The outside walls had windows where you went to get different foods. People walking by began to notice line-ups all around the building. They would become curious and come over to see what was happening. Many would stop to sample the food. The fad was beginning!

As business got busier, the brothers looked for ways to speed up the way they prepared the food. They tried new technology. A man named Ray Kroc began the big McDonald's chain. He paid the brothers so that he could use their ideas. Then, Mr. Kroc sold franchises. This means that other people could open restaurants called McDonald's. If you have a franchise, the menu cannot be changed unless all the other restaurants do the same. Think about McDonald's. What do you notice that is the same no matter what McDonald's you go to? The parts that are the same have to be the same. These are the rules that Mr. Kroc made. This is so that you can count on the restaurants when you go to them.

McDonald's in London, England is as popular as it is in Calgary, Canada.

Ronald McDonald is part of the plan to make people want to go to McDonald's. Ronald McDonald is very important to the McDonald's image. Clowns are supposed to make us feel happy and to help us have fun. That is what Ronald McDonald is about. One of the things Ronald does is give the message that eating at McDonald's is fun. Do you remember the ads on television that said, "Food, Folks, and Fun?" Do you think this was a good ad for McDonald's? Why do you think this?

McDonald's did three important things to make the fad work. It found a way to make the food quickly. It told us it would be fun. It made the restaurants work in a way that we could count on them to be the same no matter where we went.

INTERVIEW & SURVEY

1. Make an appointment with a manager of a McDonald's restaurant. Ask him or her what trends and methods McDonald's uses to keep its restaurant technology up-to-date. Also ask the manager how McDonald's tries to keep its image popular. You may also want to ask the manager if he or she thinks the idea of McDonald's has influenced other family restaurants. Put your interview in your Personal Journal.

DESIGN YOUR OWN ICON

1. Design an icon that symbolizes McDonald's.

THE FRENCH LANGUAGE

Along with English, French is an international language. An international language is one that is used in many different countries. Canada has both languages as official languages. Did you know that almost half of the words in the English language come from French? In Canada, where French is an official language, France plays a very **influential role**. Here are some of the words we use in Canada that have come from France: beef, pork, dinner, art, pardon, and theatre.

The French, both in Canada and in France, love their language. French writers are important to the French people. Thousands of French poems, plays, and stories have been translated into English so that more people can enjoy them. Here is an excerpt from a French novel called *The Three Musketeers*, by Alexandre Dumas. Musketeers were soldiers. The three Musketeers, Athos, Porthos, and Aramis, befriend young d'Artagnan, who wants to become like them. In their adventures, d'Artagnan angers a Frenchman of great power, the cardinal. The cardinal wants to prevent D'Artagnan from going to England with a message for the king. Using his wiles, d'Artagnan pretends to be someone he isn't and manages to sail from France to England. Here's how he does it:

They rapidly walked to the harbour master's house, where d'Artagnan presented himself as Count de Wardes.

"Do you have a permit signed by the cardinal?" asked the harbour master.

"Yes, sir," replied d'Artagnan. "Here it is."

"I see it's perfectly in order."

"Of course. The cardinal has great confidence in me," d'Artagnan answered.

"It seems His Eminence wants to prevent someone from going to England," said the harbour master.

"Yes, a Gascon named d'Artagnan who left Paris with three of his friends, intending to go to London," replied d'Artagnan.

"Do you known him personally?" asked the harbour master.

"Who?"

"That d'Artagnan."

"Yes, I know him very well," replied d'Artagnan.

"Then give me his description," said the harbour master.

"I'll be glad to."

And d'Artagnan gave a detailed description of Count de Wardes.

"Is there anyone with him?" asked the harbour master.

"Yes, a servant named Lubin," d'Artagnan replied.

"We'll be on the lookout for them. If we get our hands on them, His Eminence can rest assured that they'll be taken back to Paris with a strong escort," responded the harbour master.

"If you do that sir," said d'Artagnan, "you'll have earned the cardinal's gratitude." . . . Five minutes later they boarded the ship.

■

EDITORIAL

1. *The Three Musketeers* has been translated into English so that you can read it. What is your opinion? What story would you like to have translated so that others could read it?

YOUNG AT HEART MUSIC

Have you ever thought some music is just for adults and other music is definitely for kids? For many years, young people your age have wanted music that they felt belonged just to them.

Around 1950, most music was on records called singles. These records had one song on each side of the record. Country music was very popular and so was a newer style called rhythm and blues. Rhythm and blues was music that had come from the young Black people in the southern United States.

In the United States, young musicians saw a way to bring country music and rhythm and blues together. Eventually, they created a new style called rock'n'roll. The sound of rock'n'roll was influenced by music that had

Today, music is recorded on compact discs. These are a little smaller than the old singles, yet can hold 10 to 20 songs!

been around for a long time. The lyrics were written with young people in mind. Rock-'n'roll has changed since. Now people of many ages listen to it.

In this chart, the group or soloist is listed in the decade that they first hit the charts. The group's nationality will be in brackets next to its name. Although you cannot tell from the chart, many Canadians were group members of some of America's top rock-'n'roll groups.

ROCK'N'ROLL CHART

1980s	1990s
Prince (American)	Mariah Carey (American)
Bryan Adams (Canadian)	Nelson (American)
Madonna (American)	Wilson Phillips (American)
Michael Jackson (American)	Sinead O'Connor (Irish)
Janet Jackson (American)	Lisa Stansfield (British)
George Michael (British)	Black Box (Italian)
Paula Abdul (American)	
U2 (Irish)	
Whitney Houston (American)	
Alannah Myles (Canadian)	
Guns n' Roses (American)	
Jeff Healey Band (Canadian)	
Colin James (Canadian)	
New Kids on the Block (American)	

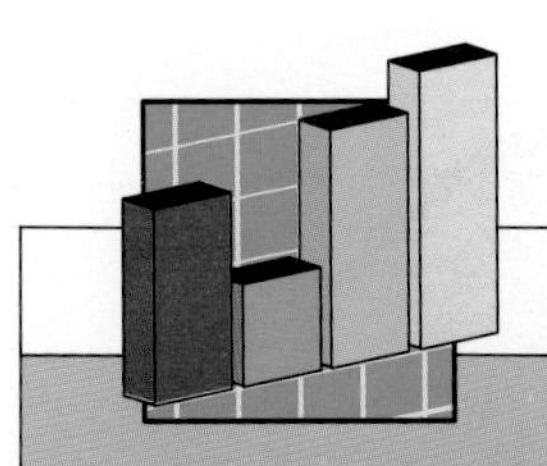

CHARTS & GRAPHS

1. Use the chart to identify some of the musicians who contribute to rock'n'roll. Which countries seem to have the most influence on rock'n'roll today?

T-SHIRTS

Would you believe that there are links between rock'n'roll and fashion? Do you own a T-shirt? Probably you do. As you read, look for the main points that show what links are a part of the history of the T-shirt. This is just a tiny part of the many ways influences in our lives come to be linked.

T-shirts were made for men to wear under their shirts for warmth. The T-shirts were plain white and made of cotton. They cost about 50 cents. T-shirts were made a part of the uniform worn by American soldiers during World War II. They were still worn under the shirt.

Young people in the United States changed that in the 1940s. Teenagers began to wear T-shirts. They did not wear the T-shirts under another shirt. Instead, they wore them as a shirt.

In England, the Beatles were starting a new trend in album covers. Most album covers at that time showed the title of the album and a picture of the person singing. The Beatles were the first to connect pictures with their music. Before long, the new idea started on the British album covers showed up in the United States. Teenagers in the United States were great fans of the Beatles. They put the Beatles album idea together with their new T-shirt fashion.

New technology in the United States made it possible to put **transfers** on T-shirts. Wearing a picture, a cartoon, or a **slogan** made wearing T-shirts very popular. It was

Originally, T-shirts were worn under shirts. Today, T-shirts show messages and art!

American teenagers who made T-shirts a part of fashion by putting pictures on their white T-shirts.

Today, it is popular to wear a message on T-shirts. In the 1990s, T-shirts are being worn by people of all ages. They are sold on every continent of the world. Some T-shirts are fun with colours. Look at the selection of T-shirts on page 80. Do you recognize the many ways T-shirts are being used to influence us?

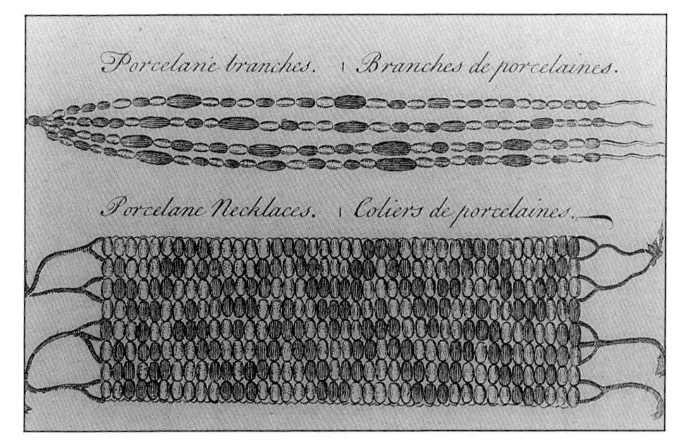

Museums have collections of art. What is your favourite museum? Why?

THE ARTS

Do you recall meeting Stanislas Renoir in chapter 3? His great-great-grandfather was Pierre Auguste Renoir. Renoir was one of France's great painters. France was, for many years, the Arts capital of the world. Painters from all over the world went there to study painting. The styles of painting in France have influenced many Canadian painters. One Canadian painter, Emily Carr, went to France to study painting. You will read more about Emily Carr in chapter 6.

Have you ever heard the expression *the Arts*? Drama, mime, music, dance, painting, and writing are all part of the Arts. The Arts are one way individuals and groups share their culture with the world. Cities in Canada, Great Britain, France, and the United States usually have museums, auditoriums, and galleries where people can enjoy the Arts. Libraries are in many communities and they are home to the stories and poems of the world.

Canadians are adding to the Arts. The Arts of Canada are shared in our own country and they are shared around the world. Sometimes this happens when museums exchange displays. The displays could be of beautiful beadwork, paintings, or photographs. Sharing of the Arts also happens when individuals or groups travel to perform in other countries. Many musical groups and dance groups travel. For example, the Arête Physical Comedy Troupe of Calgary was invited to London, England to act out a mime performance for Queen Elizabeth.

THE ARTS IN CANADA

Sculpture is one form of art. Soapstone carving began with the ancient Egyptians thousands of years ago. Today the Inuit of Canada's Arctic are thought to be some of the finest modern carvers of soapstone. Their sculptures have become an important part of Canadian culture.

Ballet is another form of art. Dancers train for years so that they can stage beautiful performances. Music, dance, and skillfully designed sets and costumes are combined to bring a story to life for the audience. The National Ballet of Canada is the largest ballet company in Canada. It performs all over Canada and all over the world. This picture shows Karen Kain, perhaps the most famous Canadian dancer ever.

Festivals also bring people to Canada. Every winter, in February, people come together in Quebec City. They come for the Quebec Winter Carnival. It takes people on an imaginary trip back into the history of French Canadians.

REPORT WRITING & OUTLINING

1. After you have reviewed the section on the Arts, create your own Arts potpourri page for each country. Use your school library to find information on the Arts in each of the countries.

CHAPTER WRAP-UP

Communication allows people to share ideas and information. One of the most basic ways to communicate is through language. Languages borrow words from each other. As we have learned to use technology like satellites to help us, we are able to communicate over long distances. Ideas from cultures of different countries are one kind of information that is communicated.

Young people can be influenced by communication links with other countries. One way this happens is through the ideas that are shared about how to use leisure time. In modern times, food, holiday time, music, and clothing have been influenced through links between countries. At first, new ideas are fads. Depending on the decisions we make, fads may last long enough to become a permanent part of our lifestyle. In the next chapter, you will read more about the influences Canadians have on the rest of the world. Canadians are world watchers, but the rest of the world watches Canada too!

ACTIVITIES

PERSONAL JOURNAL

In your journal, try one of these activities or an activity that your teacher suggests for you.

a) Write about a way in which you have been influenced by advertising. Decide if you fell for the ad or thought the idea through before you let it influence you.

b) Can you use a chart or graph to show how many of your classmates have been influenced in what they wear? Research one of these fashion trends. Try to find out where the trend began.
   - blue jeans
   - sunglasses
   - parka coats

c) Can you remember a time when you became linked with another country through the Arts? Can you think of an artistic way to retell what happened? Write your plan in your journal.

DESIGN YOUR OWN ICON

Design your own icon to show a fad. Describe the fad and who was influenced by it. Give your opinion about the fad.

CHAPTER

6

CANADIAN CONTRIBUTIONS

PREVIEW PAGE

Throughout this book we have looked at the connections between Canada, the United States, Britain, and France. Our shared history and our technological, cultural, and communications ties have influenced each country. It's important to realize that positive relationships between people and countries means that there must be some giving and taking on both sides.

In this chapter, you will read about Canada's wonderful contributions to the well-being of the world. You will read about Canada's influence upon and role in space technology, sports, politics, the Arts, medicine, and science.

CANADA IN SPACE

When Captain Kirk first said, "Space, the final frontier," we actually knew very little about what lay in space. The television series, "Star Trek," and the newer, "Star Trek: The Next Generation," are fictional. Both of these series have been successful for many reasons. One reason is that people in many parts of the world are very curious about what really is out in space. This is especially true of the people of North America.

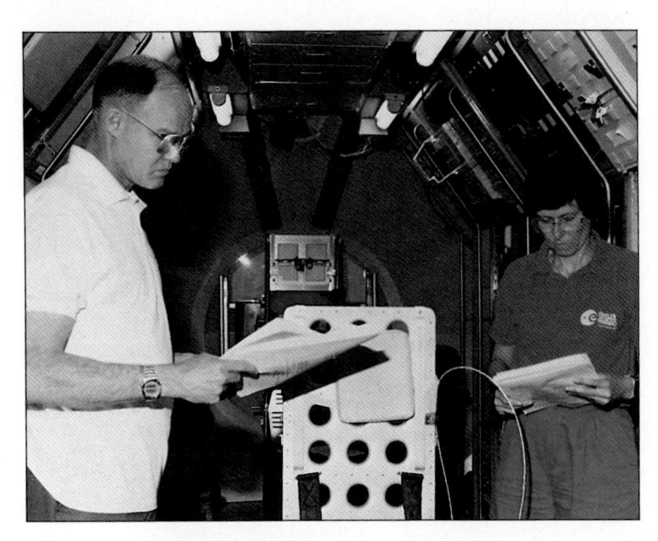

Ken Money and Roberta Bondar are Canadian astronauts. Since the 1930s, Canada has been actively exploring space.

Canadians were among the first people to become curious. Canada became a part of the space industry in its early years. New technology was needed to explore space. Many Canadians have been a part of designing the new technology. The timeline below will be helpful as you read about Canada's contributions to space.

SATELLITES, ROBOTICS, AND THE SPACE STATION

Are you wondering what all the names in the timeline stand for? Read on! *Alouette 1* was Canada's first step into space. This was a scientific satellite. It was sent to space to help scientists learn about the gases that surround the Earth's atmosphere. *Anik A1* meant that people all over Canada could communicate through satellite. Today, radio, telephone, and television signals reach all parts of Canada by satellite.

Canadarm is one of Canada's most famous contributions in space. Canadarm is a mechanical or robotic arm. It lifts satellites from the cargo bay of a space shuttle and puts them in space. Some of the satellites are bigger and heavier than a city bus! It can also

TIMELINE

CANADA IN SPACE

Date	Event
1930s	Canadians study the Northern Lights from the ground
1962	*Alouette 1* research satellite launched
1972	*Anik A1* communications satellite launched
1981	Canadarm travels to space on the American space shuttle *Columbia*
1984	Marc Garneau is first Canadian astronaut in space
1994	Launch date for *RADARSAT*

repair satellites while they are still in space. When Canadarm unfolds in space to do its work, you can see the Canadian flag and the word Canada printed on the arm.

Canadarm is a robotic arm used in space. The Americans use the Canadarm to help them work in space.

RADARSAT is a seeing satellite. It can see through clouds and even darkness! Information from *RADARSAT* can help Canada and other countries in many ways. It will be able to see what is happening with weather at sea. Ships will know where to travel to move through ice. Fishers will be able to avoid being caught in dangerous storms. *RADARSAT* will also give valuable information about our natural resources. This will help us in planning to use our resources wisely.

Space Station is expected to be working before the year 2000. Canadian scientists are responsible for designing a robot for Space Station. The robot is called the Mobile Servicing System (MSS). The MSS will have many jobs on the space station. They will include moving equipment and supplies around Space Station and releasing and capturing satellites. Canada will have an astronaut on board Space Station for 6 out of every 24 months. When on board, our Canadian astronauts will carry out space research for Canada.

USING CHARTS

Study the chart below. It shows how Canada is working cooperatively with France, Britain, and the United States on space projects. Canada is also working with Japan, Sweden, and the Soviet Union on projects. Can you see projects where Canada has worked in partnership with England? With France? With the United States? Can you find the projects where Canada joined with two international partners? From this chart, what country do you think Canada is most closely partnered with? Why might this be?

PROJECT	Canada	France	Great Britain	United States
Alouette	•			•
RADARSAT	•		•	•
*SPOT**	•	•		
Canadarm	•			•
*SARSAT**	•	•		•

* *SPOT* is a French remote sensing satellite and *SARSAT* is a search and rescue satellite.

CANADA IN SPORTS

Participating in international sports is an excellent way to bring different cultures together. People of all ages like to take part in sports. Talking about sports is almost as much fun as taking part! After the ball game, it's fun to talk about the last touchdown, or the final goal.

PERSONAL JOURNAL

1. Write a brief history of the Pan-American Games and the Commonwealth Games in your Personal Journal.

Hockey is considered Canada's national sport, but did you know that stick and ball games on ice were played in the northern part of England? British soldiers brought the concept of hockey to Canada in the early 1800s. This is another example of how countries influence each other, and of how the past indeed affects the present.

Canadian-born Wayne Gretzky is such a world class hockey player that his nickname is "The Great One." What contribution do you think a sport like hockey gives to society?

Sports events are supposed to be friendly competitions between teams or individual participants. Canada acts as a host to sports events. Also, Canadian athletes travel to compete in sports outside of Canada.

The Olympic Games in Calgary brought people from all over the world to Canada.

In chapter 3 you read about the Tour de France. This great cycling event brings people from all over the world to France.

The Olympic Games is another event that brings athletes together from all over the world. As you read, you will see how the Olympic Games is an example of a partnership and how the past has influenced the present.

CALGARY 1988— A CANADIAN CONTRIBUTION

Canada has been one of the countries of the world to support the Olympic Games. One way Canada has shown support is by hosting the games. When you host an Olympic Games, you make sure you have the buildings and sites needed for the competitions. Plans must be made to have the time of the games seem like a festival. You also invite the people of the world to come to your country to participate in peaceful competition. Canada has hosted two Olympic Games. Montreal, Quebec hosted the Summer Olympic Games in 1976. Calgary, Alberta hosted the Winter Olympic Games in 1988.

Calgary has become known for a special way that it held the Olympic Games. Thousands of people from the city became volunteers. They spent many hours helping to prepare for the games. They also worked hard during the games. They made sure that the games were successful for athletes and for the people who came to see the games. Volunteers are not paid for the work they do. They give their time to support something they believe in.

England, France, and the United States also have been hosts to Olympic Games. Along with Canada and other world countries, they share the belief in *Olympism*. Olympism is the belief that it is important to be the best you can be. The challenge of Olympism is to the body and to the mind. People who believe in Olympism work to send a message of understanding and peace between people around the world. They celebrate their message every four years with the Olympic Games.

The following photographs show how the Calgary Olympic Games were an example of the symbols of peace.

The Olympic torch is now carried from Olympia, Greece to the host country. The flame reminds us of the first games in Olympia. It is also a reminder of the ancient rule of peace on the way to the games. The Petro Canada Olympic Torch Relay began at the Temple of Hera in Olympia, Greece. The torch was lit and then flown to St. John's, Newfoundland. Then, 6500 runners carried the torch for 88 days to reach Calgary. It arrived in Calgary on the day of the opening ceremonies.

Flags are symbols that play an important role in the Olympic Games. At the opening ceremonies, the athletes of each country enter the stadium walking behind the flag of their country. The flag of Greece always comes first. During the ceremonies, the Olympic flag is raised. The Olympic flag shows five different coloured rings. The rings stand for the continents: Africa, Asia, Australia, Europe, and North and South America. The rings overlap to show togetherness.

MARK TEWKSBURY, AN OLYMPIC ATHLETE

Mark Tewksbury talks about being an Olympic athlete in this interview.

Athletes from our country participate in the Olympic Games when they are held in other countries. This is another way of showing support for Olympism. Mark Tewksbury is a Canadian who is an Olympian. This means he has participated in the Olympic Games as an athlete. Read this interview to see how the idea of peace and friendship works among the athletes.

Q: Mark, what made you want to be a part of the Olympic Games?

"I remember starting swimming when I was very young and dreaming about competing in the Olympics. I had watched the Montreal Olympics on the television and was fascinated

by the number of athletes competing from all over the world. I was spellbound at the excellence displayed by the champions and the courage and sportsmanship shown by those who were defeated. When I saw a Canadian standing on the medal podium, receiving an Olympic medal, and I watched as the Canadian flag was being raised I felt very emotional. I realized the Olympics were very special. Every four years the world's best athletes come together to peacefully compete against one another and to represent their country. I wanted to be a part of the Olympics."

Q: You began your Olympic journey a long time ago. Can you tell us how it turned out?

"Today it's 14 years later and my Olympic dream came true. It wasn't easy but in 1988 I qualified to represent Canada in the Summer Olympics held in Seoul, Korea. Competing in the Olympics was even better than I had dreamed! Not only did I get the chance to race the best swimmers in the world, I had the opportunity to become friends with many people from around the world."

Q: How has being a part of the Olympic Games influenced you?

"The Olympics, and what the Olympics symbolize, have changed my view of the world. I have learned through my competitive experiences that whether you are Canadian or French, Russian, German, or British, we all share common beliefs. As athletes, we all share the Olympic dream. That is shown through our commitment to practice, competition, and aiming for excellence. You know, many athletes started from all around the world, but we are the few that made it. We stand not just for ourselves. We stand for all the athletes in our countries who are aiming to be the best that they can be."

INTERNATIONAL PARTNERSHIPS

By entering an international partnership with other countries, Canada is able to work cooperatively with them. How do you think this benefits the countries who work together?

Canada has formed many international partnerships. The partnerships are for different reasons. Learning about space and working in space is one way Canada is a member of an international partnership. In this chapter we will talk about some other ways that Canada works as a partner in the world. You have had the opportunity to see how Canada supports world peace through sports. Now you will have a chance to see how many world countries have joined together to solve problems. This is done by an organization called the United Nations. As you read, think about how each partnership benefits the people of the countries involved.

CANADA IN THE UNITED NATIONS

From 1939 to 1945, many countries around the world went to war for a second time. World War II was so serious that even the Olympic Games were cancelled. When the war ended, many countries met to discuss ways to keep peace. They formed an organization called the United Nations. Canada, England, France, and the United States have been members of the United Nations from its beginning in 1945.

During meetings, the member countries decided that there were many ways they

AGENCIES IN THE UNITED NATIONS

Agency	Year Formed	Purpose
Food and Agriculture Organization (FAO)	1945	Works for more and better food in the world
United Nations International Children's Emergency Fund (UNICEF)	1946	Works to solve problems of health, hunger and education for children
World Health Organization (WHO)	1948	Works to bring better health to more people
International Atomic Energy Agency (IAEA)	1957	Works for peaceful uses of atomic energy

could help the world if they worked together. They organized themselves. One way they have organized is into agencies. Each agency works to help improve a problem in the world. The chart above shows some of the agencies of the United Nations and what problems they try to solve.

Did you notice that the agencies were formed in different years? Why do you think this happened? The chart above shows just a few of the many agencies that are a part of the United Nations. What do you think some of the other agencies might be?

UNICEF

UNICEF is one of the agencies shown on the chart. Perhaps you never thought about it, but you may be linked to this international partnership. Have you ever carried a UNICEF box? Perhaps you know of someone who has. Maybe you have put money in one of the boxes at a corner store or the grocery store. Many people support UNICEF by buying Christmas greeting cards. The profit from these cards goes to UNICEF work.

UNICEF was formed in 1946 to help the children of Europe and China. They needed food and clothing and medicine after the war. For four years, this was what UNICEF worked on. The people of the United Nations realized that other children in the world needed help. UNICEF has continued to work for children all over the world. If there is a disaster like an earthquake, UNICEF is one group that sends help. Help also goes to children in poor countries. Sometimes it sends equipment and medicine for health clinics. It may help train teachers in countries that do not have many teachers or schools.

If you collect for or give to UNICEF, you have become linked to children all around the world. When UNICEF began, it gave food, clothing, blankets, and medicine to children who needed help after World War II. Today UNICEF money is used in many more ways.

UNICEF money goes to children around the world. Through UNICEF, Canada gives to children who need help.

Canada has a long-standing reputation as a peaceful country, and as a mediator between countries in crisis. One of Canada's prime ministers, Pierre Elliott Trudeau, worked on peace treaties between countries. He was awarded the Albert Einstein Peace Prize for his work during 1983 and 1984. Another former prime minister, Lester Bowles Pearson, was given the Nobel Peace Prize in 1957. He had tried to bring peace to the Middle East.

Every day, many Canadians influence other people in our world. They do this by working hard to become the very best they can possibly be. You might have a special talent that will allow you to influence other people one day. Earlier in this chapter you saw how groups of people made a difference. Now we will look at just a few of the hundreds of Canadians who have made contributions to the world.

CANADA IN ARTS AND ENTERTAINMENT

Canada has many people who have contributed to and influenced worldwide arts and **entertainment industries**.

For many years Canadian artists were influenced by European art. By the 1840s, Canadian painters began to slowly introduce their unique style to art. There was a famous band of artists called the Group of Seven. They made Canadian painting well-known. Some of the best known names from the group are A.Y. Jackson, Tom Thompson, and F.H. Varley. Emily Carr and David Milne were painting at the same time as the Group of Seven, but their work did not become well known until much later. Emily Carr was influenced by European and by Canadian art styles. She became famous for her landscape paintings and for paintings that showed Native life. Artist Paul Kane also made a name for himself by painting the rugged beauty of the West Coast along with the Native people who lived there. David Milne painted country life in Canada.

Today, Canadians are proud of their artists. There are Canadian painters and sculptors who are known around the world. Our artists have their own unique styles, but they watch to see what they can learn from the other artists of the world. Perhaps you know of the work of a Canadian artist, Lynn Johnson, who writes and draws the comic strip, "For Better or For Worse." Artist Bob Carmichael designed Canada's loonie coin. Inuit artist, Kenojuak Ashevak had her print called "Enchanted Owl" chosen as the design for a Canadian stamp.

Emily Carr was a Canadian painter. She studied painting in the United States, Great Britain, and France!

Canada is also known for its talented writers. Have you read *Frozen Fire*, *Long Claws*, or *Wolf Run*? These popular books about life in the Arctic are written by Canadian author and illustrator John Houston. If you check your library, you might look for a good read by one of these Canadian authors: W.O. Mitchell, Martyn Godfrey, Jan Truss, Farley Mowat, or Monica Hughes.

Music in Canada really has variety. We have rock'n'roll, country and western, folk music, and of course, the music of our many cultures. Travel to Quebec and you will hear the lively music of the spoons. One of our most famous Canadian musicians is David Foster, who composed the theme song for the Calgary Olympic Games in 1988. Perhaps you know the music of Bryan Adams, Bruce Cockburn, Celine Dion, Joni Mitchell, or Rita MacNeil: Canadians all!

Joni Mitchell is a Canadian singer who now lives in the United States. Her songs are popular all over the world.

Do you know what these film and/or tv stars have in common?

- Genevieve Bujold, movie star
- Raymond Burr, "Perry Mason"
- Lorne Greene, "Bonanza"
- Margot Kidder, *Superman*
- Michael J. Fox, "Family Ties" and *Back to the Future*
- Donald Sutherland, movie star
- William Shatner, "Star Trek"
- André-Philippe Gagnon, singer

They were all born in Canada!

Canadians love the Arts, entertainment, and cultural festivals—and for good reasons. These activities bring different cultures together and promote a sense of being Canadian. Festivals are often the first place that creative and talented Canadians can meet the public. Some famous Canadian festivals are Heritage Days, the Montreal Jazz Festival, and the Fringe Festival.

CANADA IN SCIENCE, TECHNOLOGY, AND MEDICINE

Public personalities are given a lot of attention and can have influence over our lives. There is another group of people who have influence on our present and future lives. They are people who work in medicine, advanced technology, and in science. Think about it for a minute . . . in one **generation**, the world has benefited from inventions and discoveries such as televisions, microwaves, polio vaccines, kidney and heart transplants, antibiotics, nuclear power, and space travel.

Some famous Canadians whose discoveries, inventions, or public commitment have made the world a better place are:

- Dr. Frederick Banting and Dr. James Bertram Collip, co-discoverers of **insulin**. Their discovery of insulin has helped millions of people suffering from the disease called **diabetes**.
- Alexander Graham Bell. He invented the telephone.

Dr. David Suzuki is known worldwide for his efforts to save the environment.

- Joseph-Armand Bombardier. He invented the snowmobile.
- Scientist William Harrison Cook. His work helped **convert** freighters into refrigerated food ships.
- George Klein. He is considered by many people to be Canada's top inventor in the twentieth century. His extensive work as a design engineer includes designing wind tunnels and fitting skis onto aircraft (which led to the US Weasel army snowmobile). He was the chief consultant on Canadarm. He invented a **retractable** Canadarm. He invented a **retractable** radio antenna called STEM. It was used in space by the *Alouette 1* satellite, and is now part of standard space technology.

CHAPTER WRAP-UP

This chapter shows how Canada uses international partnerships with other countries. These partnerships allow countries to work together in ways that will benefit the people of their own countries. International partnerships often work for the good of all of the world's people. Some partnerships allow us to bring together the best research and technology. Others work to show what a good life should be for all people in the world.

Individual people can also influence our lives and the lives of people in other countries. Canadians have made many contributions to life in our world. They have made contributions in science and technology, in sport, in the Arts, and in medicine. Canadians also make contributions in other parts of life. Perhaps you can think of some examples.

ACTIVITIES

EDITORIAL

Try writing an editorial. Take a stand that expresses your opinion about Canada participating in an international partnership. Choose one of the partnerships from this chapter or write about another partnership that you know about.

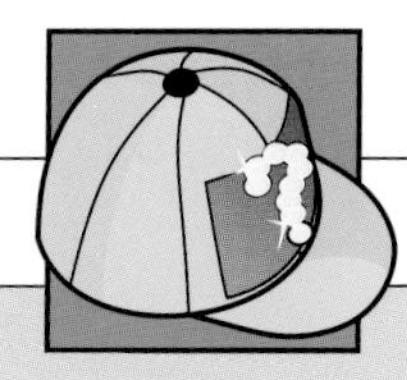

THINKING CAP

Combining knowledge and opinion in an interesting way can be a challenge. Have you ever noticed that some people are interesting to listen to when they are speaking? Usually these people have learned how to summarize their thoughts. They will often state their opinion, in a calm and confident way. Here are a few tips that can help you prepare to speak to others.

Decide on the main ideas that have to be told. Know more about your topic than what you say. Be sure of your opinion and be ready to support it. Speak slowly and clearly. Don't read! Look at your audience. Give a time for questions.

As you have read this book, you have learned a great deal about connections and how they can influence people. Pick a topic that you have learned about and that interests you. Spend some time reading and thinking. Then talk to your classmates for one minute about your topic. If you need to talk for longer than one minute, go ahead!

PERSONAL JOURNAL

1. Meet with a classmate. Discuss what you have learned about Canada's international partnerships. What do you both see as advantages and disadvantages of partnerships? After you have finished talking, each of you can summarize your discussion in your journals.
2. Look through magazines and newspapers to find an example of a Canadian who is making a contribution to our world. Write about why you think this person is making an important contribution.

How would you like to make a contribution to the world as a Canadian? Describe what you would like to do. Make a plan for how you might begin to work toward your goal. Write the plan down in your journal.

GLOSSARY

Something that is **adopted** has been taken or chosen as one's own.

Agencies are organizations that act for another person, company, or country.

Allies are nations or groups that unite for a special purpose.

Ancestors are people from whom one is directly descended, such as one's father, mother, grandfather, or grandmother.

Architecture describes the style of a building or the way it was built.

Attached means connected to something.

Beliefs are what people think is true or real.

Beset means attacked on all sides.

Borders are the lines separating two or more countries.

A **botanist** is a person skilled in studying plants and plant life.

Boundaries are like borders; they mark the dividing line between countries.

Cardinal directions are the four main directions of the compass: north (N), south (S), east (E), and west (W).

Coast is the seashore—the land along the sea.

The continent is the mainland of Europe.

Convert is another word for change.

A movie is **co-produced** when two or more people or organizations make it together.

Corduroy bridges are bridges surfaced with logs laid crosswise.

Courtyards are spaces enclosed by walls, in or near a large building.

Land that is **cultivated** is prepared for growing crops. It has been ploughed, planted, and cared for.

Cultures are the sets of customs and arts of nations or groups of people.

Customs are long-established habits.

Descendants are people born of a certain family or group.

Destinations are places to which a person or thing is going.

Diabetes is a disease in which the digestive system is unable to absorb normal amounts of sugar and starch.

Disease means sickness or illness.

The **empire** is referring to the British Empire. The empire was made up of overseas territories claimed by Great Britain.

Enabled means to give a way to do something.

Entertainment industries are all those organizations that work to interest, please, or amuse people.

Factory is the historical name for a trading post. The person in charge of the post, the representative of the trading company, was called the factor.

Factual information is not made up, it is true.

Fashionable is another word for stylish.

The **first peoples** is a name given to Natives because they were living in this land before anyone else.

A **generation** is about 30 years.

Goods are things for sale.

Green means not dried, cured, or otherwise prepared for keeping.

Gumbo is a soup thickened with okra pods, which come from okra plants.

Hearths are fireplaces.

Independent means not being connected with other countries.

Influence is the power people or countries have to act on others to change them.

A country has an **influential role** when it has the power to affect the behavior of other people or countries without using force.

Innumerable obstacles means a very large number of objects are in the way.

Insulin is a hormone produced in the body that enables the body to use sugar and other carbohydrates.

Interaction is the way that people or countries act on each other.

An **interdependent relationship** is one in which two or more people, groups, or countries rely on one another.

A **lagoon** is a pond or small lake connected with a larger body of water.

Lifestyle means a way of life, including typical habits, activities, and attitudes.

A **link** is a connection or tie between two or more things.

Livelihood is a means of living; a way of obtaining the money necessary to buy food, clothing, and shelter.

Loyalists are people who came to Canada because they were loyal to the British monarchy during the period when the Americans were wanting independence from Britain.

Material goods are physical, or touchable, objects.

A **Metis** is a person of mixed blood, especially a person of French and North American Native ancestry.

Middlemen are traders or merchants who buy goods from producers and sell them to a retailer, or directly to the consumer.

A **monarchy** is a government by or under a monarch. A monarch is a person with supreme power, called a king or queen, or emperor or empress.

The **New World** is the western hemisphere.

The **North Atlantic Treaty Organization** (NATO) is a group of nations who work together to defend themselves. The organization was formed in 1949. Among its early members were Canada, Great Britain, France, and the United States. France ended its participation in NATO in 1966.

The **Old World** refers to Europe, Asia, and Africa.

Operas are plays that are mostly sung, usually with costumes, scenery, and an orchestra.

An **opinion** is a belief based on judgment rather than knowledge; what one thinks.

Oral means spoken.

A meal that **originated** in Canada was invented or begun there.

Patriation means to bring the government under the direct control of the Canadian people.

Perishable means liable to spoil or decay.

A **plantation** is a large farm or estate on which crops such as cotton, tobacco, and sugar are grown.

A **positive influence** is something which works to change others for the better.

Potlatches are festive gatherings by Natives of Canada's West Coast.

Predicted myths or stories tell of something that will happen in the future.

Public personalities are individuals who work with people, or whose work is widely publicized.

Quitted the wagon means to get down.

Raw materials are substances in their natural state, before being manufactured, treated, or prepared.

Reserves are pieces of land set apart, usually by treaty, for the exclusive use of groups of Native people.

Retractable is something that can draw back or in.

A **revolution** is a complete, often violent, overthrow of a government or political system.

The **Riel Rebellion** occurred in 1885 in what is now Manitoba. Louis Riel organized a group of people to resist against the authority of the government.

Self-government is government of a group by its own members.

Shetland wool is a fine, strong yarn spun from the wool of Shetland sheep. The wool is often used to knit shawls and sweaters.

A **slogan** is a word or phrase used as a motto, or to advertise something.

Suburbs are the residential sections near a city or town.

Supersonic means having a speed greater than that of sound in air (about 1200 kilometres per hour at sea level).

A **surplus** is an amount over and above what is needed.

Systems of measurement are sets of ways to measure size, amount, and distance.

Ties are like links or bonds and hold things together.

Transfers are ways to convey a drawing, design, or pattern from one surface to another.

Treaties are agreements between groups or nations.

Unique means having no like or equal.

INDEX

continued

CREDITS

Editorial: Nancy Mackenzie, Melanie Johnson, Cathie Pritchard, Leah-Ann Lymer
Typesetting & Design: Pièce de Résistance Ltée., Edmonton, AB
Charts & Graphs: Pièce de Résistance Ltée., Edmonton, AB
Maps: Pièce de Résistance Ltée., Edmonton, AB
Illustrations: Pièce de Résistance Ltée., Edmonton, AB
Additional Illustrations: Page 14: Mitch Stuart, Sherwood Park, AB
Lithography: Color Graphics Alberta, Ltd., Edmonton, AB
Printing: Quality Color Press, Edmonton, AB
Index: Gardner Indexing Service, Edmonton, AB
Excerpts and/or Adaptations:
Johnson, Pauline. "The Lost Lagoon." In *Pauline Johnson: Her Life and Work*, by Marcus Van Steen. Kent, Great Britain: Hodder and Stoughton Limited.
Reprinted with permission of Hodder and Stoughton Limited.
Photos:
Abbreviations
HBCA/PAM-Hudson's Bay Company Archives/Provincial Archives of Manitoba
NAC-National Archives of Canada
BPSCL/UA-Bruce Peel Special Collections Library/University of Alberta

Entries are by page number, coded as follows: T = Top B = Bottom L = Left R = Right C = Centre

Cover
TL ©R. Adlington/Focus Stock Photo
TR ©Mario Scattoloni/Focus Stock Photo
BR ©Kim Stallknecht/Take Stock Inc.
BL Bob Adamenko/ Yankees Magazine Courtesy New York Yankees

PAGE
2 R-©Athlete Information Bureau/Canadian Olympic Association
6 BL-©R. Michael Stuckey/Miller Comstock Inc.
TR-©L. Webster/Take Stock Inc.
BR-Courtesy The British Royal Mint
7 T-©M.J. Howell/Focus Stock Photo
B-©K. McAuliffe/Focus Stock Photo
8 ©PLI/Focus Stock Photo
9 TL-©Robert Fried/Focus Stock Photo
TR-©Robert Fried/Focus Stock Photo
CR-©Michael Stuckey/Miller Comstock Inc.
B-©Richard Clement/Take Stock Inc.
10 TR-Stock Editions
B-©J. Edwards/Focus Stock Photo
11 TL-©Peter Panayiotou/Take Stock Inc.
TR-©Matthew Rosenzweig/Take Stock Inc.
B-Stock Editions
13 TL-©G. Webber/Take Stock Inc.
BL-©Naomi Duguid/Focus Stock Photo
TR-©Bill Wittman/Miller Comstock Inc.
20 Courtesy HBCA/PAM From a lithograph by W. Day
24 TL-Courtesy HBCA/PAM ©Chris Grant
TR-Courtesy NAC/PA 12593
26 B-Courtesy HBCA/PAM From a 1929 Hudson's Bay Company calendar
28 B-Courtesy NAC/C 2772 From a painting by Frances Hopkins
29 BL-H82.185.2 Ethnology Collection/Courtesy The Provincial Museum of Alberta
30 T-National Gallery of Canada, Ottawa from a painting by Thomas Davies
31 B-Courtesy NAC/C 2001
32 R-The Bettman Archive
40 BR-BPSCL/UA From Edward Curtis's *The North American Indian* "At Nootka," Plate 386
41 BR-©Victoria Clary
42 R-©Victoria Clary
43 BR-©David E. Rowley/Take Stock Inc.
44 B-©Michael Yada/Take Stock Inc.
45 TR-Stock Editions
46 TL-©Melanie Carr/Take Stock Inc.
TR-©Kim Stallknecht/Take Stock Inc.
47 L-Courtesy Rufus Scrimger
52 TR-Stock Editions
53 L-Higuchi/Miller Comstock Inc.
54 B-Courtesy Air France
58 TL-Courtesy Ford Company Canada
59 TR-©Melanie Carr/Take Stock Inc.
61 T-©Steve Vidler/Miller Comstock Inc.
63 T-©Roy Ooms/Take Stock Inc.
65 T-©Dallas and John Heaton/Miller Comstock Inc.
70 BL-©Roy Ooms/Take Stock Inc.
TR-©Pat Price/Take Stock Inc.
71 TR-Doug Curran/Courtesy Great North Productions
72 B-Stock Editions
74 BL-©Comstock Inc./Miller Comstock Inc.
76 TL-Stock Editions
77 TR-©Take Stock Inc.
79 TR-Stock Editions
80 B-©Victoria Clary
81 TR-Courtesy NAC/C 100732
BR-Courtesy Lord Collection, Permanent Collection University of Alberta
82 L-©The National Ballet of Canada/Focus Stock Photo, Photo by Barry Gray
TR-©J. Edwards/Focus Stock Photo
86 L-Courtesy The Canadian Space Agency
87 L-Courtesy The Canadian Space Agency
88 B-©Athlete Information Bureau/Canadian Olympic Association
89 BR-©Athlete Information Bureau/Canadian Olympic Association
90 TL-©Athlete Information Bureau/Canadian Olympic Association
TR-Courtesy Mark Tewksbury, photo by Brian Branford
93 T-Courtesy Unicef
94 TR-H. Mortimer Lamb/Courtesy British Columbia Archives and Records Service
95 BL-©Frank Prazak/Miller Comstock Inc.
96 L-©Fred Phipps/Courtesy CBC and Dr. David Suzuki

We have made every effort to correctly identify and credit the sources of all photographs, illustrations, and information used in this textbook. Reidmore Books appreciates any further information or corrections; acknowledgment will be given in subsequent editions.